GEORGE WASHINGTON
NEVER SLEPT HERE

Book Two of the Memoir Trilogy

Giving it the Old College Try

THE GEORGE WASHINGTON UNIVERSITY

FOUNDED 1821

FROM BROOKLYN TO D.C.

WILLIAM A. GRALNICK

Barringer Publishing, Naples, Florida
www.barringerpublishing.com
Cover, graphics, layout design by Linda S. Duider

ISBN: #978-1-954396-02-9

Library of Congress Cataloging-in-Publication Data
George Washington Never Slept Here
Printed in U.S.A.

Dedication

To My Special Angel

Acknowledgements

*Special thanks to Dr. Stephen Trachtenberg,
Brother Paul Horowitz, and the brothers
of Alpha Epsilon Pi Fraternity*

PREFACE

This is why I called it what I did.

Even writing a memoir, a kind of writing that comes straight out of your head, an author often finds research must be done. That was the case in titling this book, *George Washington Never Slept Here*. It is a riff on the famous line, referred to a little further down, "George Washington Slept Here." I got curious. Did he? Where? Why? Thanks to the Smithsonian Institute for providing the answers.

Let's begin with a description of somewhere the president did sleep, and having read it, you'll wonder, as did I, if they were all the same, why he slept in so many other places. The year was 1748, and young Mr. Washington was out in the field in his quest to learn the surveyor's trade. Bedding down for the night, he wrote in his diary, "I'm not being so good a woodsman as the rest of my Company striped my self very orderly and went in to the Bed as they call'd it when to my Surprize I found it to be nothing but a Little Straw—Matted together (and) on Thread Bear blanket with double is Weight in Vermin such as Lice and fleas etc."

Rather than polka-dotting the quote with "sics," I'll mention that Washington was self-educated, had not attended the university bearing his name, or any other. The quote is his wording and spelling.

First, as a surveyor and then in the military, he slept around quite a bit, so to speak. The Smithsonian goes on, "Driven by duty to present himself to the citizens of the shaky new union, he spent the night in so many inns and private houses that the claim *George Washington Slept Here* became a real estate cliché, as well as the title of a clunky 1940 stage (and screen) comedy by Kaufman and Hart. Others reviewed the movie starring Jack Benny much kindlier."

Things did get better. Once he moved into Mt. Vernon with Martha, his brother Lawrence gave him a beautiful, sturdy bed. It still rests at the plantation. He slept in it as often as possible until his death at age sixty-seven from a sudden onset of a throat infection that stopped his breathing. Martha never again slept in it. Awwwwww.

True love for the ages (that's mine, not the Smithsonian's . . .).

Table of Contents

Introduction

TO THE

INTRODUCTION

"Itchy balls" have nothing to do with gym fungi. They are the spawn of the American Sycamore tree.

I didn't know what to call the introduction to the introduction, so I've called it the Introduction to the Introduction. "Why?" you should be wondering, "does one need an introduction to an introduction?" I am prepared to answer that.

Hard as it is for me to fathom that some of you are reading this tome without having read its prequel, I thought you might profit from an overall introduction before you get to the specific introduction. 'with me on that? Please know that enjoying this book has nothing to do with having read its predecessor, however my introduction will give you a sense of what that book covered, my style of writing, and hopefully two appetites. The first comes with this thought of yours, "Holy Hanna, Bat Girl, how did I miss, *The War of the Itchy Balls and Other Tales from Brooklyn*!?!" And you'll buy it by going on Amazon.com where you can bathe in the stellar endorsements and humbling reviews. The second is an uncontrollable need to dive right into the book at hand.

Having explained that as well as I can, I have one more explanation. What follows is three stories from, *The War* . . . each presenting a different stage of my life. I hope you will enjoy them, and they will grease your reading skids right into the main attraction. I'll also do the uninitiated the favor of explaining that itchy balls have nothing to do with gym fungi. They are the spawn of the American Sycamore tree. They start out as hard as golf balls and about the same size. On maturity, they can be almost the size of a baseball and have become soft and furry. When they touch something or someone, they explode becoming the Sycamore's version of the broom in *The Sorcerer's Apprentice*. However, to find out what place they take in the book . . . you'll have to buy it. Now, off to *The War* . . .

P.S. 217

"There's a reason my school memories start here—it's called trauma."

I vaguely remember going to a pre-school. It was in a Brownstone and downstairs. I have no memory of grades one and two. I must have gone to them because I do remember beginning grade three and I couldn't have done that without having gone to grades one and two. Right?

By the time I was school age, we were living for the second time near Prospect Park and then around the corner at 500 Ocean Avenue. When we moved from 500, we moved into a different school district and that put me into P.S. 217, one of the oldest elementary schools in Brooklyn. Its size was imposing, though almost anything of size is imposing to a third grader.

It was a big building whose front, with steps and columns, was on Newkirk Avenue, but only visitors used the front. The other three sides of the building were hemmed in by cement school yards, each with a door leading into the school. One faced Rugby Road. That's the entrance I used either through the school gate or when no one was looking, through the arch that was artfully snipped into the fence so that the school yard was open even when it was closed. That meant nights, weekends, and holidays. The other playground faced Coney Island Avenue.

The building was red (or once was) brick and had huge windows that were opened from the inside with long "window poles." They had a circle at their business ends that hooked into a metal hook at the top of the window. Some you pushed and they opened on a diagonal; some you pulled down on and they opened like, well a window. All of the windows on the first floor had full size metal grates on them from the time that the Board of Education realized that budget was more important than esthetics. Air conditioning had not been invented when this school had been built.

There is a reason my school memories start here; it's called trauma. On the first day my mother drove me, and again for several more days. We had to park a ways from the school yard. I could hear the din of line up before I ever saw the school. It was a hum or maybe a buzz. And it got louder as we got closer. We crossed Foster Avenue, continuing on Rugby. There were on the school side several older houses; across the street was a large apartment building directly facing the school yard and side of the school building. When we passed the last house, there was nothing between us and the din but that chain link fence, I almost croaked. With nothing to block the noise, it turned into a low roar like what came from a sea, an ocean, but these sounds were made by kids, swarms of them.

Intermingled were teachers yelling, "Grade whatever, Mrs. So and So over here." Some also had signs. It looked like a miniaturized labor rally. Into that mass of humanity, I was to go, stopped at the gate by a teacher who said something like, "OK, Mom, say your goodbyes. I'll take it from here." She politely asked me my name and I impolitely burst out crying and almost ripped off my mother's dress as I grabbed for her. She had begun to move away, and I was terrified. Kids remember stuff like that.

I survived, got to my place, and ended up in the right class. It wasn't moments after I got settled when someone came and announced that Billy Gralnick was wanted by Miss Bildersee. Not enough time had passed for me to have done anything wrong that would land me in the principal's office; I didn't know she had a policy of personally meeting all students new to her school. Nor did I know that this Johnny Cash of principals, always dressed in black, was a legend in New York City education, as had been her family for generations. In fact, I didn't even know she was Jewish until a few years ago. She looked more like an old-world, Sicilian mourner except for the pince-nez perched on her nose.

I have no idea what she said to me besides "Hello, Welcome to P.S. 217" and a lot about rules and behavior. I had this sixth sense that I was about five feet (the distance between our chairs) from real danger. I couldn't wait to be given a hall pass, a piece of wood about the size of a brick, that had "Pass" etched into it, and looked like it had been around since the opening of the school—along with Miss Bildersee. I was now escorted back to class; the pass was over-kill except the rules said . . . My escort threw open the classroom door, announced, "Mrs. Kimmel, this is Billy Gralnick," and suddenly I felt like spotlights had gone on in class and they were all focused on me. Anonymity, so craved for, was not to be mine. Finally, I was assigned a seat; I got to sit down.

Never would a school desk feel so safe again. While the teacher did her roll book, I lost myself in imagining who belonged to the names inked, carved, and otherwise scratched into my wooden desk. None said RIP, so a little bit of hope began to rise within me. I did in fact make it to the closing bell. Day one was in the books.

Aunt Pauline the Pencil Lady

"In a word, he was cheap. In two, he was very cheap."

Everyone has an Aunt Pauline, regardless of her name. She's that spinster aunt who loves you dearly but can't quite remember which birthday it is you're celebrating. She takes you places you don't really want to go and gives you things you don't really want, but she smells nice and means well. My Aunt Pauline didn't stay a spinster forever, but we're not there yet.

The second oldest of my father's four siblings, Pauline was sort of mannish looking, also prim and proper. Unlike her older sister who was short, stout, and had a bosom that could confound a bra saleswoman, Pauline looked more like a tennis player. As the family was hit harder and harder by the Great Depression, Pauline became more and more "Papa's girl" as she worried about his long hours and financial struggles. This pattern became her life after her fiancé committed suicide by jumping off the Brooklyn Bridge during the Great Depression, something my brother and I as teenagers found inexplicably funny. When my grandfather died, she threw herself into caring for her nieces and nephews, of which I was her favorite.

There were things she'd take me to that she was sure I would love that I didn't, like the annual church bazaar on Eastern Parkway across from The Abraham Lincoln Apartments where she lived for decades. There were other things that I hated then but came to realize were wonderful things to have done with her like the Brooklyn Museum visits and concerts at the Brooklyn Academy of Music. The Museum had this amazing display about American Indians that I remember to this day, and I heard *Peter and the Wolf* for the first time at the Academy. It remains today a seminal memory; I still have the 78 rpm with Basil Rathbone (real name!) narrating.

The thing about Aunt Pauline was that she was a little weird. She never forgot my birthday, but for years the number on the card was always a year or two off. And always too young. Maybe she didn't want me to grow up. Usually, her birthday presents were also off, more appropriate for the age of the card she sent than the age I actually was, but her strangest ways manifested themselves in for-no-reasons gifts of pencils and dollar bills.

Whenever we had the family over, Aunt Pauline would come in and whisper to me that she had something special for me. Each time, that special thing was a bunch of #2 pencils that she had used and sharpened back to a point. Thus, they were both used and of varying lengths. What she thought I would do with them, especially after she'd given me about a pound and a half of pencils, I don't know. But they just kept on comin'. The other gift brings us to the end of her spinsterhood.

My mom was the advisor to all the women in the family on whatever problems they were having or whatever decisions they had to make. Years after Uncle Murray, the furrier, died and Aunt Pearl met Harry, the whatever, who asked for her hand in marriage, she was on the phone and then in the house in record time. What to do? What to do? Mom said marry him. She did.

And so, it came one day that Aunt Pauline decided her dull, dark apartment needed a new lamp. She walked down the block a ways to the lamp store and there she met its owner, Izzy Pollack from Wales. Izzy was about the size of a gnome, had ears like Dumbo and was immediately smitten with my aunt. He sold her a lamp and then pursued her like a golden retriever puppy pursues its playmate—relentlessly. Now it was Pauline's turn in mom's chair because he asked Pauline to marry him. And with mom's assurances it was the right thing for her to do, she did, leading to one of the most hysterically funny nights in our family history.

It was a simple wedding conducted by a rabbi in the chapel. We had a reception at our home and afterwards Iz and Pauline left to spend their wedding night together at the Abraham Lincoln Apartments. No honeymoon. Iz was in a word cheap. In two, very cheap. Both I guess in their fifties at the time, the tennis player and the gnome took their leave from all the well-wishers and disappeared into the night. At about 1 a.m. the phone rang. It was Pauline—screaming.

In trying to calm her down, my mother woke everyone up. When she finally got Pauline calm enough to understand what had happened, this was the story. All the cabinets in the kitchen, full of dishes and glasses and whatnot, had fallen off the wall in what must have been the likes of the cymbal crashes ending the *1812 Overture*, scaring them both awake and half to death.

Now they were faced with a disaster scene. Abraham Lincoln Civil War-like destruction was to be found in his name-sake apartments in Brooklyn, NY. Just no dead bodies. A brigade was needed. All hands on deck. We all dressed and drove over there and no lie, there were cabinets everywhere, some smashed on the sink, some smashed on the floor, pieces of plates and glasses, large and small, exploded over everything. You know of course what my teenage brother and I conjured up in our minds as we envisioned what the tennis player and the gnome could have been doing on their honeymoon night to shake the cabinets off their moorings . . . so we laughed until we almost wet our pants.

As I said, Izzy was cheap, so cheap that he made the proverbial Scotsman seem generous. Someone said, "He squeezes the nickel so tight, it makes the bull shit." For instance, eventually everyone in the family had new lamps, but Izzy's idea of a gift was a deal—

10% off. Or if it was a really good lamp . . . five per cent. Free? Not in his vocabulary. So now we come to the second of Pauline's gifts.

I think my mother had tipped her off that I had enough pencils to run an art studio and she could start throwing them out rather than wrapping them up. "Well," she asked, "what do you give a boy?"

"Money" was the answer.

Came the inevitable family party and now Aunt Pauline has a husband, a cheap one. As usual, she greeted me with a whisper, "I have something for you." Later in the day, I saw her scope out the room to see where Uncle Iz was located. When he was far enough away, Pauline would pull me into a corner and slip something that felt like origami into my hand. It was a dollar bill, always folded as many times as one could possibly fold it then pressed into my palm with this admonition: "Now don't tell Uncle Iz . . . you know he loves you but . . . you know how he is. . . ."

"Yes, I do," I would think, "cheap!"

And so, unfolds the story of Aunt Pauline and her origami dollars who lived longer than Uncle Iz and I think ended up with more money than he had, and certainly more pencils.

Sharon

"He wasn't wearing a gun because he was a cop . . . he was a killer."

Some dates with girls hold a place of their own. This is the story of one. It includes, the Mafia, jailbait, and stupidity drawn of naiveté. The "jailbait" that my brother picked up at Coney Island, who looked seventeen but was thirteen, he decided would help me earn my spurs. Yee haw!

Not even close.

He had prepared me for our joint venture to the beach. "How are we going to find one girl amidst a million people," I asked with a hopeful twinge of defeat in my voice. He responded, first she's always in the same spot and secondly . . . you'll know."

Gulp.

She was in "her spot." And yes, I knew. How to describe what I saw? A reddish blond girl sitting on a blanket. One leg was outstretched, the other bent at the knee. Her arms were up behind her head as she slowly, very slowly stroked her long hair up on top of her head. To do this she had to arch her back in an incredible curve, not incredible because of the arch, incredible because of what the arch did for her chest. This girl was for me? I thought I would die—of a heart attack. My brother said, "I told you. Now go talk to her."

"Go talk to her" was more of a command than a suggestion and it came with a shove. I could embarrass myself in front of my brother or embarrass myself in front of this goddess. It was a hard shove and physics solved the dilemma. There I was, at her blanket. She knew I needed help, so she opened with, "You're the brother, aren't you?" "Yeehss, I stammered." "Hi, my name is Sharon, pull up some blanket and sit down." Also, more of a command than suggestion. She was not sitting on a beach blanket the kind that are traditionally the size of small bed sheets. She was sitting on a towel and sitting next to her was really being next to her, close enough so that the sweat pouring out of every pore of my body mixed with her suntan lotion, the application of which was the close of her show, as she slowly, ever so slowly rubbed it up and down outstretched limbs and . . . you get the point, I'm sure.

What transpired post introduction was idiot talk. She wasn't the going-in-the-water type. My mouth was so dry I needed the ocean to swallow and just as I figured all was lost and said, "I guess I better be going." She said, "Aren't you going to ask me out?" Damn! Almost forgot that part. So, I did. "How about Saturday night?" The next question I should have been shot for: "You like to bowl?" "Sure, why not?" she responded. I had a week to prepare for the disaster that was going to occur but let me tell you why I should have been shot.

I had no car. I had no idea how to get to where she lived. Nor did I have any idea where there was a bowling alley in her neighborhood. I had set myself up for failure and boy did I ever succeed.

Back in the day, local directions were obtained using telephone books and telephones. I looked up "Bowling Alleys" in the Yellow Pages. Mind you, telephone books in New York were so big and heavy they were used as door stops, car seats for women who couldn't see over the steering wheel, and a host of other things not connected to phone numbers. I picked what seemed to be the closest and called for directions. We would have to take a city bus. How cool is that . . . ? Not. The only good news was the bus stopped in front of her apartment building and in front of the alley. A cab you say? My parents offered nothing towards this outing; I would be lucky to have the money I needed for the bus rides and the bowling.

Then I got directions from my brother as we both prepared for our Saturday night dates. I said, "Should I kiss her goodnight?" His flat, scornful response, "No schmuck, shake hands." I got the point.

Aside from getting slightly motion sick on the bus, the trip to her apartment building was uneventful. That is where "uneventful" left the stage. I knocked on the door. Her mother answered, and I was greeted like she had never seen a clean cut, freshly scrubbed kid come to pick up her daughter. It was an effusive greeting—a little overwhelming actually. She took my hand and said, "Come. Let's see if Sharon is ready." Again, a command, not a suggestion.

I thought there would ring out from her mouth in her oh so Brooklyn accent a call like, "Sharon? Bill's here. You ready?" and a response would return through the bedroom door. "Not quite."

She pulled me across the apartment to Sharon's bedroom, knocked once and in the same motion flung open the door. Sitting in front of a dressing table mirror was Sharon in a state I'd call definitely not ready. While her back was to me, the mirror gave a full-frontal view of pulchritude in bra and panties. With no particular alacrity did she pull up her dress, sitting on her lap, to cover herself. She smiled and cooed, "Hi! I'll be ready in a few. Mom close the door." Speechless, that was me.

A few minutes of small talk later, she made her entrance. She was wearing a herringbone jumper that some artist had painted on her between the time her mother and I exited the room and she made her entrance. This dress had straps that went over both shoulders, each with a black button that buttoned right on top of her nipple, like a pasty on a stripper, except she was wearing a blouse underneath. One of these pesky buttons kept unbuttoning during the evening. It was all very disconcerting. As we left the apartment and waited for the elevator, I said," You look great, but are you sure you can bowl in that outfit?" "We'll see, won't we?" she said in what was the first time I had heard "sexy" in a voice directed at me.

Came the bus and the next event—getting up the stairs. Initially there were two people struck into stone by what they were seeing. One was me, behind her. The other was the bus driver who had a front row seat in front of her. It was something to watch. I was so transfixed and so zeroed in on being a gentleman that I began to walk her to an open seat, with every riders' pair of eyes, male and female, fixed on her, that I forgot to pay.

This booming voice rang out, "HEY KID. THIS AIN'T FREE. YOU PLANNING TO PAY?" So, I got her settled and in a very unsettled state, I walked back to the front to face this very large, black, unhappy human being who thought he was dealing with a wise-guy rather than a kid who was in way over his head.

To compound things, being a subway rider, I had no idea what the bus cost, so I handed him a bill. He snapped, "Change only. 'goes in the hopper." The hopper was about a two-foot-high glass container that had indented slots onto which you threw your money. The machine separated nickels dimes and quarters while making these very mechanical noises. I asked how much, reached into my pocket, and threw in the exact change. Remember, I said it counted nickels, dimes, and quarters? You didn't read pennies and pennies were all I had to make up the fare. He was not a happy man but had to drive his bus. "Go sit down!" Another command.

But he wasn't done with me. He must have been watching me in his mirror because as I got to where I had seated Sharon, holding the metal hand holders attached to the aisle side of each seat to steady myself on the rocking bus making its way down Nostrand Avenue, he hit the brakes—hard. He hit them just as I released one seat handle and was reaching for the next. I was catapulted forward into that handle, which was at crotch height. To say I oozed into the seat next to Sharon breathless and sporting a color on my face not found in the large size Crayola box wouldn't be exaggerating much.

Not much transpired on the bus because I was looking out the window hawk-like for our stop. You had to see it before you got to it, reach up, and pull the bell cord or the driver would pass it. For sure this driver would be making no exceptions for me. I spied. I pulled. He stopped. This time we exited the bus from the rear, giving those paying passengers the show they had missed on our entrance.

And there it was in all its neon glory, the bowling alley. We walked to the desk to pay for games to be played and over to the other side of the desk to get our bowling shoes. Each attendant gave Sharon a very quizzical look, sort of an unsaid, "You know we don't have changing lockers here." We soldiered on.

I went first, managed to knock down a bunch of pins and impressed her with a spare. I helped her choose a ball. She bent to pick it up and "pop!" went the button. One strap now waved to and fro across her chest. She took the ball, did her run up, and threw it into the gutter. "Maybe you better help me on the next one." I'll save you the reading, just imagine sex between animals. While it probably didn't happen, at the moment I approached her from behind, the lights in the place went up, the sounds of balls-hitting-walnut wood ceased, pins stopped dropping, and the setting machines stopped setting. Everyone was again looking at us. I think we got through three games and two cokes before calling it a night.

I was terribly preoccupied on the bus, so preoccupied that having seen the opening of her act, having watched her make her body do things almost unnatural as she tried to bowl, and seen her get on the bus, the finale wasn't too distracting. I had "the kiss" on my mind. Apparently, so did she.

I had it all worked out. We'd take the elevator to the fifth floor. At the fourth floor, I would turn, embrace, and kiss her. This unfortunately was not her plan, which was to hightail it off the elevator, cut left, fly down the hall and kiss me good night in front of her door.

Being nervous, my timing was a bit off. I missed four. As the doors opened at floor number five, I turned to embrace a girl who had flown by me and was on her way to her apartment. I was astounded. I was now in hot pursuit, but the doors, beginning to close, hit me like two line-backers, one from each side. When the rubber protrusions on the doors are hit, the doors jerk to a stop, so the passenger isn't squashed. As loud as in Dolby Stereo came a sound. It was "ka-chunk, ka-chunk, kachunk!" as the doors tried their best to shut. Finally, I untangled myself from these willful monsters and raced after Sharon who was already in position in front of the door, eyes closed, lips pointed upward. As I closed my eyes, reached for her waist and puckered my lips—the door opened.

No longer was I greeted by the effusive Mama Bear. There stood Poppa Bear. He was wearing shirt and slacks. Under the arm he used to open the door, hanging below his armpit, was a .38 caliber pistol. Teenaged boys know these things. In one smooth motion, he snatched his daughter and thanked me for what he was sure was a lovely evening and shut the door. Just before the doors closed, out slipped the words, "Call me."

So, I did and here is a postscript. Sharon invited me over one afternoon to hang out with her friends. I met her on the corner wearing my standard chinos, sneakers and t-shirt, what you wore just in case a basketball game broke out in front of you somewhere, sometime. Sharon, dressed as only Sharon could, was surrounded by motorcycles that in turn were surrounded by, to borrow a word from my mom, hoodlums. Suddenly, I understood Mama Bear's effusive welcome to me on our date.

I learned two things as I gingerly interacted with the players on the set. One was that a very stand-offish guy who looked like carpenter nails were his afternoon snack, had a crush on Sharon and it would be better for my health if I didn't develop one too.

The second thing I learned was that Poppa Bear wasn't wearing a gun because he was a cop. He was a killer, a captain in the Mafia.

I saw Sharon once more at the beach, but the thrill had been replaced by fear and but for a few phone calls more, dim the lights the party was over.

But the worst of the worst? Sunday morning, I had to explain to my inquisitive brother, act by act, the play that was our date. He listened impassively, and turned away, muttering . . . "Hopeless . . ."

*"I have a deep, deep love
for sneakers."*

– Kerry Washington, actress/
activist Phi Beta Kappa, double
major, 1998

*"A University . . . in the Nation's Capital . . . to which the youth
. . . of the Nation . . . might be sent . . . for their Education in . . .
polite literature . . . arts and sciences . . . in politics . . . and good
Government . . ."—George Washington*

Introduction

My experiences probably are not too different than yours
. . . it's just that I see them through a "different" lens.

This book is the second in what might become a three-part memoir. It follows, *The War of the Itchy Balls and Other Tales from Brooklyn*. That work took the reader from about year three to year seventeen in my life. This one covers college.

George Washington Never Slept Here is written with the same philosophy as its predecessor, that there's pretty much no such thing as an ordinary life. Oh, there are some, but the trick of finding life interesting, as opposed to mundane or annoying, is how you look at it. Even though I come from Brooklyn, my experiences probably aren't too different than yours, no matter where you're from. It's just that I see them through a similar lens as did Woody Allen, Buddy Hackett, Don Rickles and so many other more famous than I Brooklynites. The stories however are universal.

You may not have gone to college, but you were once the ages of those that did. Age has a lot to do with what happens to a person and how that person feels about them. This book will begin with that awful year, one which begins with college board tests, arguing with parents over the different schools you and they have picked, the dreadful wait to hear from any one of them from either list, and will take you up to my acceptance to The George Washington University.

So, folks, turn the page and let's begin wandering through the next stage of my life.

Enjoy!

". . . alternate facts . . ."

— Kellyanne Conway, White
House counselor Trump
administration, honors
graduate, Law Center, 1992

*"Making a speech on economics
is a lot like pissing down your leg.
It seems hot to you, but it never
does to anyone else."*

– Lynda Bird Johnson Robb
(a quote from her dad),
daughter of President Lyndon
Johnson, first lady of Virginia,
attended GW with the author

PART ONE

Leaving

the

Nest

Introduction

Going to college, or not, is one of the biggest decisions one makes in life. It's right up there with that first job decision. It is complicated—emotionally, financially, and educationally. For the vast majority of high schoolers, it meant leaving home for a long time for the first time. Even then, it was expensive, and many families had to balance finances against the best education they could afford. It hopefully meant a ticket to a good job so long as you graduated. It was the beginning of an awful eighteen months for some like me and their families.

THE CHOICE OF WHERE TO GO

"Half of what you learn," he said, "is learned outside the classroom."

Two around-the-corner-neighbors had a great impact on me, one in my freshman year of high school, the other in my junior year. They get pre-college kudos.

The first was Dr. Gupta. Related to CNN's Sanjay? No idea. I do know that Gupta is a common Indian last name. For me, his first name was doctor. Dr. G. got a dog. It was the same time I had a gig as an old-fashioned apprentice to an old-time veterinarian. No pay but until I had an allergy attack and lost a career at fifteen, I experienced almost everything that could be done to a small animal, from ear cleaning to major surgeries. Back to Dr. G. He was a surgeon and decided he would spay his pup by himself. He said to me, "want to tag along and assist?" Oh yeah!

It was fascinating but what I learned from this was if you can do it, do it. Have a little gumption. When we were in the operating room at a local hospital, I said to him, "Are you allowed to do this?" He replied, "I'm a surgeon, I have privileges at this hospital, this is my operating room. Seems alright to me." Of course, today he'd never get away with it, but then the whole deal spoke to me.

One door down from him was Dr. Lindsey Perkins. He was a southerner and spoke like it. Oddly enough, he taught English at Brooklyn College, which was about 100 feet from my high school, Midwood. AP students, of which I was one, could take college courses from their professors. I went to GW with nine credits in my pocket. Perkins was a friendly guy, had long ago acclimated himself to being a white, Anglo-Saxon, Protestant, southerner living in a Brooklyn, Jewish environment, and while he had no kids, he had great intuition about their problems. He sensed I was having a very difficult time at home. We struck up a mentor/mentee relationship.

Time came for me to take my PSAT's. The results indicated strongly that I needed a prep course. Had my scores been any lower, they would have been on the other side of the paper. I took the course and then took the SAT's. My scores went from shockingly low to just low. Here, I was an honor roll student, enrolled in college courses, from whom my parents expected great things and the College Board folks were hinting that maybe I should go to trade school. My being a writer has great irony to it. I think I got a 450 in English. Math? I won't even tell you. Fortunately, there were the afternoon achievement tests on which I did above average but no Duke Snider home runs by any stretch of the yardstick. I was one of those kids who just couldn't take standardized tests.

There was additional weirdness. I took the New York State Scholarship test, a standardized test. I didn't understand half the questions, no less feeling like I answered most anything correctly and yet . . . I won a state scholarship. As our current president would say, "Here's the deal." I could go to any college in the state, tuition free, almost a full ride. Or . . . I could go to Brooklyn College for a completely full ride because I'd live at home. The parents were so hep to that idea that they offered me a car and an apartment. I didn't believe them. Now enter Dr. Perkins.

I had applied to all the schools I should have and one I shouldn't. You'll have to read *Itchy Balls* to find out how that worked out. Michigan, from which my brilliant cousin had graduated with honors, and gave to generously, was our big hope. Its acceptance record over the years, showed a real love for Midwood students of which it took a disproportionately high number annually. Annually, that is, until my class began to apply. It seems those who preceded what I hoped would be me, got involved in a cheating scandal. They got thrown out and Midwood students were blackballed for a few years.

Number two hope was Rutgers. My great aunt had donated hundreds of acres of land on the Raritan River, instead of leaving it in her will to us. My mother had another cousin who owned the still famous "21" restaurant in New York. He was on the Rutgers Board. The icing on the cake was that my mom was a graduate. Maybe the fix could be in. I applied. Word came back at a restaurant lunch full of rich, famous people none of whom cared about where I went to college. I however was sweating bullets. I was told, "You're gonna get in." Delirium overtook our table. Then came the next lunch.

Rutgers was a state school. It had very strict limitations on the number of out of state students it would take in a year. With a perennially awful football team, it had the chance to grab a right tackle from the middle of the country. They took him instead of me. So much for the fix being in. Then came the letter to slam the door with finality. I didn't go to Rutgers but I did get to eat at a restaurant that most people couldn't even get a reservation for. La de da.

Dr. Perkins commiserated with me through these traumas. He urged me to keep applying. "Don't go to Brooklyn College," he would opine. "You'll get a fine education, but you'll be going to college with the same kids you went to high school with even though most of them will have different names." Home grown wisdom. Out went more letters, in came more rejections, until . . .

WILLIAM A. GRALNICK

You have to have been a Republican to know how good it is to be a Democrat.

– Jacqueline Kennedy, former First Lady, United States of America, 1959

"It's about finding your values, and committing to them. It's about finding your North Star. It's about making choices. Some are easy. Some are hard. And some will make you question everything."

– Tim Cook, CEO Apple,
DHL 2005, quote from
commencement address 2005

The Letter

When that letter came, I knew I would be terrified to open it.

The rejection letters began to arrive. I had received that New York State Scholarship. It began to look like my choice would be an in-state school out of New York City without the promised perks of Brooklyn College. Then the letters from the others began to arrive.

Once upon a time, people used to write post cards to one another. Mostly, I guess, they were from vacation spots but often enough they were just short letters. Post cards were cheaper than envelopes by several cents. I wished that universities replied by post card. Why? Because our mailman had the habit of reading everyone's post cards and saving them work by giving them a synopsis as he handed them the mail. Sometimes, if it was one sheet of paper written in dark ink, an envelope didn't thwart his civic duty. When that letter came, I knew I would be terrified to open it. I wished Sol could just read the card and deliver the news.

It was a small envelope with a picture of George Washington and the name The George Washington University. I was in hyperventilation. They liked everything about my submission except my board scores. They understood that not every student tested well, even good students. If I were willing, they would give me a provisional acceptance pending an interview. I was willing.

I took the bus to DC and a cab to school. I have no memory of what building I went to or even if I was interviewed by a man or woman. That's how nervous I was. I do remember being seated in a chair that pushed up against an old-fashioned radiator. It was winter, bitter cold. I was wearing a heavy, grey, wool suit. The radiator was spitting out steam and in minutes beads of sweat began to roll down my spine and minutes later those beads became a small lake which turned my shirt into a blotter. The blotter stuck firmly to my back. I was so uncomfortable I don't remember the questions or the answers but apparently, they were a lot more impressed with me than I was. Right then and there they intimated I was in, a proud Colonial, and the letter would follow confirming it. It did. I was going away to school, a good thing for all.

Getting ready for college is like getting ready for summer camp only more so. This is packing for a year not a summer. The other difference is the college doesn't send you a list of what to pack. That was the dawning of the reality that college is not only different from camp but radically different from high school. No one I met arrived without clothing; many arrived with too much. One freshman girl brought fifty pairs of shoes and at that she left a bunch more home. I was stunned. Well, the car got packed and mom, dad, and I filled up whatever space was left and headed out of Brooklyn to the New Jersey Turnpike and I-95.

Here's another major difference, the one between the first day of elementary school and the first day of college. They are mirror images. When the parents say goodbye at elementary school the kids cry; when parents say goodbye at college the parents cry. In the school yard, children's hands became coated with super-glue as they clutch whatever part of their mothers they can grab. In college the student is straining credulity trying not to say, "GO ALREADY!" as the parents linger finding just one more thing to arrange, one more piece of information forgotten to be told, one more hug to be given. Finally, they left with my firm promise that every Sunday morning around 11 a.m. I would call home and in between I would write at least once a week. Sounds like camp.

My father wrote me that they had to pull off the highway at one point, so they didn't kill themselves trying to drive through the tears. Me? I was like a puppy let outside for the first time off the leash. I ran in circles, jumped up and down, ran up this street and down the other. I would have barked if I could have. And mind you, I hadn't gone up to my room yet. College officially begins with the leaving of the parents and the realization that you are going to be living in a room three times the size of a closet with another human being unrelated to you, and, who in the normal course of life, you would never even have met. We will meet him in due time.

Parting Is

(OR ISN'T)

Such Sweet Sorrow

"I couldn't get out of the car fast enough . . ."

It was time to go. The trunk had been shipped, the car was loaded, shortly Waldorf Court was as they say, "in the rear-view mirror." We wove our way out of Brooklyn to I-95. Disjointed, uncomfortable, halting conversation filled the car. Mostly it was dead silent. My mom was map master. She had the trusty Triple A TripTic in hand and having made but one pit-stop, it got us to my next home, Adams Hall.

When my wife and I took our daughter to GW, we were there for several days. We almost dropped dead getting stuff up to her room in the dormitory that had been built while I was on campus and in whose lobby, I was to meet Loreli (that's foreshadowing). We went to dinner. We had breakfast together. We spent hours helping to arrange her one-fourth of a tiny room. Eventually, we hugged goodbye and left for home. That day, years before, when our car arrived was nothing like what I just described.

I couldn't get out of the car fast enough, through the dorm doors fast enough, and up to my room at the same speed. Conversation had ground to a halt. We had already covered "being careful," the importance of doing homework and studying well in advance for tests. I'm not sure "have a good time" ever made the list. Finally, after exhausting every possible piece of advice, warning, and reminders about changing underwear daily, we hugged and kissed goodbye, my mother burst out crying. I was amazed. It was the first time it had dawned on me that this was something momentous in her life as well as mine. Moments later Adams Hall, my dorm, was in their rearview mirror.

I was thrilled. I was on my own.

It was time to go see what this college stuff was all about.

Skip's Fan

"Skip"

Twenty-four seven the fan whirred, no matter the temperature.

I almost exited the elevator before the door opened. My room, it turned out faced it. I knocked on the door. No answer. I knocked again and was met with a "yeah?" That was my introduction to Horace Winston Meister. I said, "Hi!" I'm Bill Gralnick." He said, "Skip." He'd already claimed the real estate he wanted. We were not off to a great start.

Over time, or even in our daughter's day, our room was comparatively huge and there were only to two of us in it. It had three separate spaces: a study alcove with two desks, the sleeping area, into which one walked upon entry, and the bathroom replete with private shower.

Over time my roommate became more conversational. He was American, born in North Carolina, his dad was an executive with Mobil Oil; he was raised in Venezuela and spoke Spanish fluently. He had wispy, blond hair, blue eyes, and became a magnet for homosexuals one of whom he found in his bed when we came home from a party.

Eventually, I would be the first Jew ever to set foot in any house his parents lived in. Through thick and thin, we became stalwart friends and stuck together all the way through college. Until we matured a bit, we would spell each other calling the multiple dates we made for Fridays and Saturdays. We'd whittle down the list to one and then I would call his other dates and give them an excuse and he would do me the same favor. His first girlfriend was Jewish, and he pledged with me my Jewish fraternity, Alpha Epsilon Pi. We competed with each other on who could do the best meringue and he was forever ticked off that my grades in Spanish always bested his.

Sacrosanct in Skip's life was his fan. I saw it at his feet when I walked in the room and continued to see it at his feet while studying no matter what place we occupied. It mattered not winter or summer. It was his "white noise" and his version of Linus' blanket.

When young men bond, the bonding takes on different phases in different ways. Our most notable moment was a real lesson in life . . . a Jew Hater. He etched into our door, "we got six million the last time, we'll get more next time." (Think "past is prologue" and then think Charlottesville, Va.). We were pretty drunk when we got to the room and were confronted by the signage on the door.

I don't know why we darkened the room. Probably because the light hurt our eyes. We began having a pretty dark conversation, no pun intended. He was quizzing me about things Jewish. At about 2 a.m. I said to him, "Skip, if they came to the door and said 'we're here for the Jew,' would you fight them or let them take me?"

After a pause, he said, "take you." I was crushed but I had sense enough not to react. He was who he was and I liked him so I let it be. But the Lord works in mysterious ways. I told you his first, college love was a Jewish girl, very New York Jewish, Long Island to be exact, and he joined a Jewish fraternity. Upon graduation, he switched his registration from Republican to Democrat, he went from social conservative to social liberal and so went the metamorphosis of my roommate.

PART TWO

Settling In

Registration: Everyone needs good deodorant.

Introduction

It takes even less time than setting up one's summer camp bunk than to set up one's room in college. One reason is that in camp counselors are looking over your shoulder. Like the Army, the Sergeant barks and the recruits listen. In college, nobody cares if your clothing is folded, which drawer what goes in, if it hangs color-coordinated in the closet, or even if it's clean. Another is that you can't wait to get out of the dorm and see this new land you've arrived in. Is it *Brigadoon* or *Dante's Inferno*? Let's start with the building the room is in.

The Dean: Bark and bite were equal.

Dorm Life

To say strange things happen in a dorm is to understate the case.

In a sense, living in a dorm is like living in an apartment house, but . . . That "but" is way more important than the words that precede it. For instance:

. . . but in apartment houses, the tenants lock their doors and stay put. Not in a dorm.

. . . but in an apartment house, people can go days or months without seeing other tenants especially those on other floors. Not in a dorm.

. . . but in an apartment house, most of the people leave and return at about the same time. Not in a dorm.

. . . but in an apartment house, there is a superintendent, and that person does things like cut down dead animals someone hung from the fan in the elevator. Not in a dorm and a good place to begin.

To say that strange things happen in dorms is to understate the case. Let's begin with the animal. One night at the end of a bender someone who happened to live on my floor had a thought. It was the kind of thought drunk people have. It struck him as being funny if he took his lab animal, a fetal pig, tied up its legs and tied the other end of the rope to the elevator fan, so the pig was literally in your face as the elevator door opened.

But there's more, so much more I hardly know which to regale you with next. Should it be coffee and tea, should it be lemonade and pee? Should it be love by beer can or love by electro-shock? Maybe we'll start with the blanket and the church bell.

Behind Adams Hall there was a stately Protestant Church. About a stately three stories high, its stately bell tower would sound the call to the faithful every Sunday morning in a most stately and loud way. That would be early Sunday morning. Regardless of faith, the residents on the third floor, and for that matter that whole side of the building were none too pleased. Most of them were not wrestling with God; most of them were wrestling with hangovers for which the bell became a toll from hell.

The following piece of ingenuity makes one wonder about the future of America. It seems two guys got "brave drunk" or maybe "stupid drunk" but fortunately not "fall-down drunk." You'll see why "fortunately" in a moment. Deep into thought about how they could manage a late morning's sleep, they ruminated over the physics of bellringing. They remembered Quasimodo but knew there was no descendent of his up in the tower. One of the faithful pressed a button and the bell did its thing on its own. That meant if they could get up there, there wouldn't be a pitched battle, heathens against faithful, on the roof.

There were two problems to solve. The first, how to get up to the bell tower. The second how to silence the bell. This is where "brave or stupid drunk" comes in. They jumped. And they made it. Of course, they hadn't given much thought to how they were going to get down. It's one thing to jump from a window ledge to a roof; it's quite another to jump from a roof to a window ledge unless of course one is a squirrel or pigeon or monkey.

They also were clear-headed enough to resolve the sound issue. A bell has a clanger. Stop the clanger from hitting the bell and the bell is muted. This became a two for one mission. They took a blanket from the room figuring if they fell it would help break the fall (drunks don't think too sharply) and if they made it, they could stuff the blanket up the bell's . . . well how about wrap it around the clanger, which they did.

The caper was executed during the wee hours. Come Sunday morning, something amazing happened at the church. Nothing. Well, almost nothing. If you listened carefully enough, you could hear something like a "thump, thump, thump." But the caper still had that last detail that was not resolved so when came the thumps, came the two freshmen forlornly sitting next to the thumper.

The rest of the story isn't as interesting. It took place in the Dean of Men's Office, he who happened to be of the same denomination as the church. It involved loud voices, muffled pleas, and handwritten, long and sincere sounding, apologies. There was a threat, but it was too early in the freshman year to expel anyone.

Let's move then to "Love on a Beer Can." Rules, they say, are made to be broken. In spite of the rule that no girls were allowed beyond the lobby of the dorm, some made it, and some with some regularity. One well-hormoned, young male was making a habit of both locking his roommate out of their room and being a bed-born athlete driving the residents on the other side of the wall nuts. Why? Because the bed would bang against the wall with a rhythm that increased in tempo until it ended like the end of the *1812 Overture*—with a choir, booming canons and a big bang. This caused those residents to be: annoyed, jealous, and thinking about phrases concerning revenge.

Sometimes an idea is so off-the-wall (no pun intended) that it smacks of genius. These guys began collecting beer cans, drinking them dry of course. Over the course of several months, they accumulated a junkyard full of 'em. With good intel they found out the night and time of the next tryst. The yet to come on the scene Watergate burglars could have taken a lesson. These guys broke into the room and dismantled the bed. They unscrewed the bed's legs and then stacked up rows and rows of empty beers cans until the bed height on cans matched the bed height on legs. They then pulled down the sheets to make a makeshift whatever you call that thing that covers what on a normal bed would be the box springs.

Enter Romeo and Juliet. They had to be stealthy quiet, which was perfect. No impassioned embrace, ripping off clothing, and falling onto the bed. Everything had to be done tippy-toe quiet. Then began the banging—against the wall, you louts. But I guess the other too. As the pace quickened, the bed began to sway and at the, excuse the pun, climatic moment there came this time a real, cymbal-like crash Tchaikovsky would have been proud of, as hundreds of empty beer cans went in twenty different directions and the bed but one—down.

Genius, no? Let's call it street genius.

This next episode involved the use of real intellect and knowledge. Here, in the story about "Love and Electrocution," we meet a star-crossed lover. The object of his affection couldn't slyly slip under his covers; she was a thousand miles away. To bring her closer to his heart, he brought with him from home a large, beautiful, filigreed frame in which was a beautiful picture of this beauty that undoubtably was a going away present. He worshiped this picture like it was an altar. Now comes what we'll call the "Agatha Christie part."

He returns from class one day to find his alter overturned. The frame and its adored contents were face down on his dresser. "Probably the cleaning service was dusting it and either tipped it over or lay it down and forgot to pick it up." Ok, he could live with that—until it happened again. Then it began to happen with regularity, but without a pattern. It wasn't Monday, Wednesday, Friday. It didn't happen only Friday afternoons. He couldn't find any clue that would help him put this bloke into a public stockade or worse.

Now he had a mission. He had both to stop this sinner and teach him a lesson. But how? The moral of this story is know your enemy. Our young revenge-seeking student was studying to be an electrical engineer. His idea? Take an extension cord and strip off the protective coating. That left two strands of six feet of copper wiring. These he entwined through the spaces in the metal frame. The other end of the wire was attached to the plug. This went into a socket behind the dresser. This IED was pretty much invisible. All there was to do was wait.

If I concentrate hard, now fifty-five or so years later, I can still hear the scream.

The perpetrator became obvious. He had one helluva burn on his right hand.

And you know what? No one ever touched the picture again. Justice served.

Then we have the thirst-quenching chapter we'll call, "It's the same color but is it the same thing?"

This story's theme is much like the others. One person does something that gets on another's nerves and the other seeks to stop the action with a counter action that will also exact revenge. So here we go.

It's winter. Winter in Washington DC is a misery. It's damp, to-the-bone chilly, often wet and sometimes, as you will read elsewhere, it snows. There is, however, to the enterprising dorm-dweller an upside. The rooms had no refrigerators. During the winter, you could leave drinks of choice on the window ledge and they would be nice and cold when you wanted them. Planning begins.

In spite of what one hears about college students, drinking is one of those things about which people are particular. Some prefer wine, others like beer, still others its liquor. Take me for instance. When it comes to wine, I prefer red, sometimes a strong cab, other times a lighter pinot. When it comes to beer, I'm definitely a Guinness guy; I hate Coors. I'm a scotch man, mostly like it on the peaty side

One of the fellas in the dorm was a lemonade man. He loved his lemonade. When he could, he would make it himself. Winter was his happy time. There was no need for ice cubes that would melt and water down his libation, Nope, just put the drink on the window ledge, make sure the cap or top was on so some curious bird didn't leave a deposit on it, or in it, and the next day nothing could have made him happier. Ice cold, full strength lemonade. Go figure.

Now college students in dorms have a unique ability to scope out someone's weak spots. Rarely do they stick the proverbial knife into them. Rather they poke and probe, cut a little, twist a little. Many could have been fill-ins when some of the inquisitors were out sick or on leave. Let the word go forth that someone was in love with lemonade, almost addicted to it like some are to having that first cup of coffee, and the wheels begin to grind. They came to a halt again, and again in a fairly ingenious way. The rooms in the dorms were stacked. Had a room on the top floor collapsed it would have filled the one below and so on, until the debris got to the foundation. Thus room 504 was atop of 404. With great care and a steady hand, one could lean out of 504 and drop a line with a noose on it to the ledge of 404. And that's what they did. Come morning, up went the window, out went the hand. It came back empty. Supernatural? Magic?

OK, so it was windy, and the brew blew off the ledge. Maybe it happened again. But a few days later, when it happened a third time—suspicion was raised. The mind in 504 was not as sharp as the mind in 404. It couldn't for the life of it figure out what the hell was happening. DC has a fair share of vultures and hawks. Could they be snatching the lemonade and flying off with it? Certainly, they were strong enough. Yet no one had heard of lemonade drinking birds, or birds uncapping lemonade and feeding it to thirsty hatchlings. 'twas a head-scratcher. Ahhhh, but the mind is a wonderful thing, not to be wasted. What could be put in the bottle that would appear to be lemonade but wasn't?

The first go-round was an art class. How much yellow paint in water would it take to match lemonade? Between the drops of paint on the bottle and the endless and fruitless attempts to get a match, that plan was dropped. Besides, it wasn't diabolical enough.

Even if one is a good sort, given the drive to think evil, evil happens. The brainstorm hit. 404 peed in the bottle. True. When set on the ledge it was warm enough to give off steam. It also had a little head on it, like a long neck beer that had just been popped open. A few hours on the ledge though and those problems would disappear. Soon enough so did the bottle.

Also magic, it never happened again. Peace reigned as it should during the holiday season and winter slowly turned into spring. No more art. No more chemistry. End of story.

Stuff like this would happen all the time. It could make a person batty, even paranoid. Yet it seemed that God, like He or She does for drunks and little children, watches out for freshmen in dorms. On every floor, there was either an enforcer who could be appealed to when things got out of hand and he would threaten to break someone's arm, or there was a calmer, wiser, Yoda-like personality who was the floor-whisperer to whom one went.

My floor had such a one. I think his name was Spencer. Spencer seems like a name for a floor-whisperer. I was seventeen, he was twenty-four. He was freshman and so was I. I had one brother; he had I think fourteen siblings. My brother was five years my senior, God bless his mother and father, Spencer and his youngest sibling were twenty-some years apart. Spencer served two tours in the Navy stationed in the British Isles. His room was stocked with shelves of tea and equipment to brew it. Spencer was a great listener and a great tea-brewer. From him, I learned in times of stress nothing was better than to sit down, quiet down, and have a "cuppa."

Such is a slice of life in a men's dormitory as almost, but not quite, men lived it.

Private comment, as quoted in *Name-Dropping* (1999)
by John Kenneth Galbraith, p. 149.

*"It is better to offer no excuse than a
bad one."* . . .

*"It is better to be alone than in bad
company."* . . .

George Washington

PUT YOUR HANDS
ON THE
Radio

Jesus' tears, water from the Jordan, sins erased by radio

I guess a case could be made either way for whether college students would be expected to fall asleep as soon as their heads hit the pillow, alcohol being a sedative and all, or that anxiety over this, that, and the other thing would bode four sleepless years. For me, falling to sleep was always a slow process and sometimes I needed more help than the background noise of Skip's ever-running fan. It was on those nights that I grabbed for the transistor radio, plugged in the earphone, and slowly crawled up and down the dial until I hit gold. Gold was WCKY.

Those might not have been call letters, but that's what I remember them as. In those days, AM radio was king. There were 5,000-watt local stations mostly for farmers that kept them up to date on stuff about hogs, cows, and corn. There were also 50,000-watt clear coverage stations that on a clear and interference free night could be heard half-way or more across the country. WCKY was a 50,000-watt station with 5,000-watt listeners. After midnight on the right kind of night, it would find its way into my radio. Except years later when the parody of such things came about on *Hee-*

Haw, this was a revelation to me. Since much of what it played after midnight was good ol' hard core gospel, revelation seems to be the right word. To this Brooklyn Jew, it was spell binding.

The music was mostly rousing and all Jesus. Occasionally, the music was interrupted by "the message." A preacher would come on and level your soul with high decibel, fear inducing, old fashioned religion. Each must have gone to the Elmer Gantry School of Radio Preaching. They'd reach a fever pitch and then tell the listeners to put their hands on their radios, and the preacher would heal their bodies, cleanse their souls, make granny's bones stop hurting—all for a small donation, of course.

There was always something on sale. Vials of Jesus' tears were a popular item as were different size bottles of water from the River Jordan—and for me, albums of this family or those sisters, or the so and so gang of fiddlers. Yes, I bought them. I still have them. It was mesmerizing, until one day the newspaper did an expose on these types of shows and their preachers. Stuck in my mind is the description of the church basement filled with women at long tables opening stacks and stacks of envelopes from which money would pour and be stacked by denomination. I'm not judging, I'm just saying . . . praise Jesus.

"The cure for crime is not the electric chair but the high chair. Some days you're the kid with the stick, some days you're the pinata."

– Alec Baldwin, actor, activist, 1976-79

No matter what you needed . . .

WHY DID THE STUDENT
Cross the Road?

"What the hell was that?" I asked. He replied, "A dead chicken."

For my first night out as a free man, I decided I should grab a bite to eat, before hitting the fraternity open houses. I had heard a lot of chatter about some hamburger joint called White Castle, so Skip and I decided to try it. I knew not from White Castle, which apparently was an iconic, southern, pit stop. They served the smallest, thinnest, square hamburgers sprinkled with teeny-tiny pieces of onion set into a bun four times the size of what it was holding. There was not one thing about the food or the restaurant, which was blazing white, that would lead anyone to guess correctly why castle came after white.

Getting there was easy. Out the front door, cross the street, straight down the block. It was then that I began to learn that nothing is easy. I looked both ways, but not down. After about three strides into the street, I suddenly went ass over teakettle and found myself looking up from the street at my astonished roommate. It was bone dry outside but somehow, I had slipped. I said to Skip, who was now looking down, at me, and said, "What the hell was that?" His reply, "A dead chicken."

So it was. This poor bird was the end product of a Santeria ceremony that I later found out took place in a small church right near White Castle. Trying to divest myself of feathers and blood, and not step on the chicken's head, which was separated by several feet from its body, I went back inside, cleaned up, and off we headed for burgers and later beer. It was to portend several odd experiences, the next of which would take place on the way back to the dorm after having imbibed more beer in one night than I had had up to that time in my entire life.

Ambulances are normally not the cause for riotous laughter unless one has been playing "99 Bottles of Beer" and doing it at several different places with walls. By the time I decided to head to the bed, I was as plastered as the walls holding the beers. I don't remember too much about the parties other than there would be a few each night for a week, that there was a surfeit of pizza to go with them, that every place was packed and jammed and therefore noisy enough to be heard well before you got there, and college man or not, I still did the same thing I always did in high school when walking into a crowded mixer—I found a neutral corner and watched. Since all the corners were gone along with most everyone's inhibitions, it got easier. The more I had to drink, the easier it was to mix.

Then came the ambulance. Amazingly enough, it had nothing to do with any of the parties. The famous George Washington University Hospital was adjacent to campus so ambulances coming and going were common. I'd learned that when the windows were open at Adams Hall. What was the cause for my ribs to be so tickled? And mind you I was alone, a sole drunk staggering home. It was the ambulance's siren. I kid you not. In Brooklyn, a siren was a siren, sort of like a WW II air raid siren. Ambulances in DC hooted at you. Whoop! Whoop! Whoop! Now I'll be damned if I know why that struck me as funny. At first it didn't, but it sort of grew on me. Suddenly, I began to giggle and then I burst out into unending, belly-busting, peals of laughter. Chalk it up to the Clydesdale's, I guess. Mind you, I was doing this while not only alone but near no other human. Fortunately, when the ambulance stopped so did the siren and so did my laughter. The one thought that managed to swim into my brain was that my stupid behavior couldn't even yet be called sophomoric for here I was only two days into my freshman year.

"Terrible" doesn't come close to how I felt in the morning. I managed to dress myself and get to Quigleys, the campus everything store. Some urban planning genius had decided what could be more important to be near a university dormitory than a drug store. I walked in, approached the counterman, and before I could utter a word, he scanned me and said, "Wow!" He then reached for a bottle of Vitamin B6 and said, quietly, "This will help burn off the alcohol. Take aspirin every four hours and don't drink tonight." I don't even remember if I managed a "thank you." I decided to follow his advice. First of all, I thought if I didn't, I might die, or worse yet, keep living while feeling like this, and secondly because registration for classes was to begin and I had heard one needed to be on top of one's game for that.

I got the better end of the deal.

Registration

Worse than Sales Day at Lohman's.

Today's students know not from real, old-fashioned registration. Everything is done by computer now, and before one ever gets to school. There is no mad dash from building to building, campus map in hand, so you knew what building you were at and if it was the right one. There was no standing in lines that often snaked around things and down the sidewalk—like voting lines. There was no gut-wrenching panic when you found out the class you needed with the professor you were told to take it with was closed out. Then, uttering curses and prayers, you joined another line, sometimes in another building, and tried again. Registration was a war game, not an activity.

Once registered it, was time for the bookstore. As every student knows, textbooks are very heavy and very expensive. The GW bookstore was as full as was a fraternity house during a party. Added to the scene were student workers trying to keep the shelves full as they balanced stacks of books while running from the storage closets to the right shelves. Some had the woeful task of having to say, "Sorry, we're all out. It's on order. Check back with us in a few days." More unfortunately "in a few days" class would have started, and you would have started behind your luckier classmates who had beaten you to what you needed. Because you'd never done this before and didn't know that coming to class day one without a book didn't end life or bring you an F, it was a very unnerving experience—until you got to the next night's party and an upper classman told you neither would be the case, in fact no one ever brought books to class.

Why? The answer unlocks the secret to the biggest difference between high school and college, the reason why was in the president's address to the freshman class. He said, "Look at the person to your right. Now look at the person to your left. The odds are that two of the three of you won't be here this time next year." And why not? Not so much because some students just can't hack college. Not so much because some students can't draw a line between stupid and common sense and hadn't as yet learned as Forest Gump later told us, "You can't fix stupid." Nor because they didn't get a textbook for a class on day one.

No, it's because, if you'll pardon the French, the professors don't give too much of a crap about freshmen. They are teaching large, lecture halls and worrying about whether their just submitted paper to some academic society would be published and keep them on track for tenure. High school teachers are paid to see that you learn. College professors are paid for a lot of things, not just teaching. Whether or not you learn is your business, not theirs. They are not there for the glory of the student body, but for the glory of the university and both reputations, theirs and the school's. Not all mind you. I had a few that broke the mold. The rest seemed to be there to try and break me.

I am easily scared so I studied—a lot. I disproved the College Board's intimation that I should have gone to plumbing school. I made Dean's List first and second semester and graduated with honors. I would not be one of those who would not return this time next year.

"Whatever America hopes to bring to pass in the world must first come to pass in the heart of America."

— David Eisenhower, grandson
of President Dwight David
Eisenhower, JD 1976

Best Italian food a student could afford.

AVOIDING

Starvation

Eating in college one quickly develops a fondness for mom's cooking.

My last major learning experience before school started was how not to starve to death. I hated White Castle and my weekly allowance from home ($20!) had very little room for restaurants. I had the school food plan—another building to find, the cafeteria, and learn how this gig worked. Suffice it to say, finding the cafeteria was the easy part.

If there was a more institutional looking, less appetizing, university cafeteria somewhere, I was glad I was not going to school where it was. The same went for the mostly women who ran the place, cooked the food, filled the food compartments and handled the bookkeeping for the meal plan. They added no glow to either the setting or the food. It was soon obvious that at 135 lbs. and 6 ft. tall, I would not be gaining much weight if I ate much food at this place. And this was before the city shut it down for a bit. But I get ahead of myself.

And how could I have led such a sheltered life that I'd never been in a cafeteria that had heat lamps from under which you took your selections? Yet I hadn't. So, as I navigated the line, silly me thought the lights above the food were to help you see it. I learned quickly they were not. How? When I reached my arm in for some unappetizing something or other and ended up at the student health center with a second-degree burn on that arm from that arm playing Icarus with the heat lamp. It was the first time in my very short life as a drinker that I felt like I needed a drink. And the meal was breakfast . . .

Quite the first few days. I had learned what a White Castle was, almost dislocated my back slipping on a dead chicken, got stupid drunk at fraternity welcome parties, met my roommate and his fan, and needed medical attention from trying to feed myself.

It dawned on me, "All this and I hadn't been to a class yet!"

"We are all dishonored when a veteran sleeps on the same streets that he or she has defended."

– Senator Tammy Duckworth,
MA International Affairs, 1990

Big Joe and the Nordic Goddess' hideaway.

Joltin' Joe—
WHERE DID YOU GO?

Joe was big. Not so much tall, but big. And hairy.

This is not a dormitory story in that it involved the fraternity house. Set the scene circa 1962. That's important. In 1962, fraternity house stories were a mixture of storybook material and urban legend. No sexual abuse. No death. No trials. And at The George Washington University, with a former Army Infantry colonel as Dean of Men, things remained on the side of semi-rationality—usually. This is one of several stories when it didn't.

It is said about teenagers that they scream to be independent, but in reality, they are pack animals. The packs may diverge from the norm but everyone in them is the same. So it is with fraternities. By and large, at least in the '50s and '60s, each college fraternity had a look. One could with near certainty look at a guy and guess he was Sigma Chi or A E Pi or a girl and know she was a Tri-Delt or A E Phi. Mostly pledges were chosen who fit the look. Except for a few. My fraternity was the first chapter in the country to pledge an African American and another who wasn't Jewish . . . We had the first hippie, long-hair brother. And we had Joe.

Joe was big. He was not so much tall, but big—and hairy. He

had big, wide feet. He was bear-like. A nice guy, he had few social graces, no snappy New York sense of humor. Joe was just sort of there, there being nice. Everyone figured Joe would be the guy we'd all be trying to fix up with dates for major school and fraternity events because, well, he looked like a bear, albeit a nice one. We were wrong.

One night at a pan-Greek mixer, Joe met this blond. Nearly as big as he, she was stunning in a Norse "I'm from Minnesota" Warrior Princess way. A digression: in those days Helena Rubenstein and her colleagues hadn't yet come up with makeup products that stayed on. The song, "Lipstick on your Collar" rang true for many a guy who was kissing the wrong girl. If one were a passionate kisser one could come away from a make out session with enough transferred makeup to look like a cartoon-face covered with lip-like imprints. This is important. Remember it. Now . . . back to the story.

Sometime during the mixer, Joe and Princess Ursula disappeared into the basement. When they emerged, we knew, somehow, we had misjudged the bear. Ursula looked like someone had taken her armor and run a tank over it and Joe looked like he'd emerged from a lipstick marketing trial. For a brief moment, as they stepped into the light of the fraternity house's living room, there was a sudden oxygen deficiency as everyone sucked in their breath. With snarky smiles on their faces, the Warrior and the Bear departed. That's the prelude.

Big Joe and his princess were an item for the semester. The pattern was always the same. We all should have bought stock in Kleenex or the company that made it for the amounts Joe must have used to clean himself up. And since dates were expected to escort their girlfriends back to the dorm to check in, often under the watchful eye of a Marine-like dorm mother, the cleanup and straighten up had to be finished before curfew. It didn't take long for their passion and post-passion play clean up to become part of the norm. Until the night it didn't.

I forget what time girl's dorm curfew was. I want to say 1 a.m.

on weekends and 11 p.m. during the week. One Saturday night, the always punctual pair wasn't. By 1:20 a.m. the Marine-like dorm mommie, manning the desk of Miss Minnesota's dorm, called our fraternity. Was the Nordic Goddess there? Nope. Why this became our job, I don't know, but she told us we had an hour to produce the wayward pair or there would be hell to pay, hell to pay in the person of the Dean of Men who she would rouse from bed to be on scene.

Not a campus school, GW was fairly compact in those days. There were only so many places they could be: the fraternity house, her sorority house or nestled in the bushes of one of the monuments on the mall making Lincoln or Jefferson blush. The memorial that most matched the going's on would be the Washington Monument . . . but it had no hiding places around it. So, with the Dean and his tucked-under-his-arm riding crop in our minds, we divvied up the logical hot spots and scattered. We came up empty, so the Marine called the Dean. Another digression:

GW, especially in those days, was one of the safest pieces of real estate in the District of Columbia. First, it had its own campus police. We were two blocks from the White House, so the area was always crawling with secret service, some often at school because the kids of a lot of famous government officials, including during my years the daughter of President Johnson, were enrolled. On the other side of the school's center was what was then called the Executive Office Building. It is where the Vice President had his offices and it also held the headquarters of the police force responsible for protecting the federal buildings. Added to this were the officers whose responsibilities included protecting the memorials and finally we add the District of Columbia police force. The FBI headquarters was a mile away in one direction and Fort Myer Army base about two miles in the other. By the time the dean was done, every one of these agencies save Fort Myer had been contacted. Dragnet is the word most appropriate for what ensued. By 4 a.m., they were still no-shows and a certain gloom, tinged with fear, began to pervade our innards.

As we tell our children, every story has an ending and this one did too. A happy one if you were feeling jealous; a not so happy one if you were the bear and his warrior woman. Here it is.

Smack dab in the middle of campus was an area called the quadrangle. In its center was a spruce tree so old and so big it might well have been planted by George Washington. Its majestic boughs layered one over the next and swept right down to the ground. You could not look under the tree without lifting up these tremendous (the tree had to have an eighteen-foot circumference) boughs. Are you beginning to see the picture?

I had had it and was headed back to my dorm. I was too tired to care. They were dead or not. I needed sleep. The shortest way to my dorm was across the quadrangle. At some point, one of their mental alarm clocks went off. As I passed the tree, there came this rustling, and out from beneath it, shedding pine needles from hair and clothing, were our "two Rip Van Winkles," who, as the story was told during the interrogation, had crawled under the tree for some privacy. The ground was soft and smelled seductive courtesy of this tree having shed Lord knows how many decades of fragrant needles in a bed George Washington would have paid many pelts for. The tree was the mature participant in this saga; it had probably seen this movie before many times. Big and strong as Joe and Brunhilda were, they had been, shall we say, very active; it was late. They had worn themselves out and fallen asleep.

I on the other hand had the same fatigue without the benefits. I told them curtly they better get "the you know what" to her dorm and what to expect when they got there. I knew there was neither bounty nor reward, so I then continued to trudge towards my dorm, muttering, shaking my head, and wondering aloud, "If some guys have all the luck . . . why aren't I ever one of them."

I can't remember what punishments were meted out. I can tell you though that whatever they were, Joe was happy to suffer them, and more. After all, who goes to college and becomes a legend before his sophomore year?

FROM THE IRONING BOARD TO THE *Dermatologist's* OFFICE

I decided coming home clean and pressed . . . would be good.

Socially, especially for underclassman, it was all about getting an edge. Often, the best one could do was a suntan. Our fraternity house had a flat roof, and it was not unusual for us to be sitting up there with aluminum reflectors scorching our faces—in February.

But it started with an iron. Eventually, you have to go home. That happens just about the time you've begun to feel really independent. Came the first break in classes, Thanksgiving, I wanted to have something to show my mother that would prove I had begun to grow up into a college man. I had very few options because well, what she didn't know wouldn't hurt her, or me. I decided coming home clean and pressed rather than looking like I'd just fallen out the front door of the fraternity house after a party would be good. I took a nice, button-down shirt, swept everything off my desk, and set about ironing it. It looked pretty easy when I had watched our housekeeper do it. It wasn't and it isn't. Basically, ironing is an exercise in geometry, a subject in which I did very poorly in high school.

The back was easy. It's just an expanse of cloth. The front is trickier. It would be a lot easier if the buttons could be clipped off and replaced when done, but they can't, so one maneuvers the nose of the iron in between the spaces of the buttons and then wrinkles the back of the shirt in turning it around to get the 1" space on the other side of the buttons across from which would be the holes they go into. The collar—a challenge but doable. The sleeves—forgedabudit! Or them. Anyway I labored over this shirt long enough so that if I were running a laundry I'd have gone out of business. I put down the iron, stepped back and admired my work. Unfortunately, I didn't remember to put the iron down top up. A burning smell snapped me into awareness, and I grabbed the iron, more properly knocked the iron off the shirt. The burn mark would be lost once I tucked in the shirt.

So off I went to the train station sporting tie, sport coat and snappily ironed oxford shirt. I got home to hugs and hellos, took off my jacket, and was asked by my mother, "What did you do—sleep in that shirt?" I never ironed a whole shirt again. However, I did discover that if only the collar and cuffs were ironed and a sweater worn over the shirt, you looked golden so long as you kept on the sweater, which is what I did.

How does this relate to dermatology? It was realistic for the vast majority of us freshmen males to think that girls in whom we had interest would only see our hands and face. Thus, if we went up on the roof of the fraternity house wearing a shirt and jacket so as not to freeze and only fried our hands and face, we'd look great. And that's what we did. With baby oil and iodine were a year-round staple, winter or summer.

Let's jump four decades. My doctor said to me it's time for you to start seeing a dermatologist. So, I went. I guess I've had as many cancers removed from face, head, arms, and chest as Phyllis Diller had plastic surgeries. She of whom Johnny Carson once said, "If you took all the skin taken off Phyllis Diller you could make another woman . . ." With me, maybe Phil the Groundhog. Ba da boom. Fortunately, no melanomas—yet. But this story is another testament to *Saving Private Ryan:* "You can't fix stupid." And stupid is what you do in pursuit of girls.

Registration before computers.

PART THREE:

Fraternity Life

Introduction

A fraternity is a group or organization where members share common business or professional interests and goals. A cultural or social fraternity enhances the betterment of its members. Brotherhood is a synonym. That is why fraternity members are called brothers. Non-members often call them jerks. The origin is Greek (brotherhood, not being a jerk). That is why pledging to join a fraternity one must learn the Greek alphabet, one of the single greatest wastes of time and useless pieces of knowledge for anyone other than those studying for the priesthood in the Greek Orthodox Church.

In the charters, one finds lofty goals and ideas about service to the community, service to mankind, service to family and friends. That's in the charter. Mostly, when I was in a fraternity, fraternities were for parties and for having groups of guys who would either not call you a jerk when you did jerky things or stop you from doing them before it was too late. In the '60s, the fraternity system was almost entirely segregated, though like with Black colleges there is a great tradition in the African-American community of fraternities and sororities. They were separated also by religion. There were many Christian fraternities that didn't take Jews because well they were Jews. They also were bulwarks of anti-Semitism either overtly or covertly. So, like Jews formed their own country clubs when the shee-shee clubs wouldn't accept them as members, so too they formed their own fraternities (and sororities). Best known were TEP (Tau Epsilon Pi), AE Pi (Alpha Epsilon Pi), and ZBT (Zeta Beta Tau also known as "zillions, billions, and trillions"—a hint that classicism was also alive and well.).

For me, fraternity life as it was called, was a savior. I was seventeen and socially shy. When I was accepted as a pledge to AE Pi, it ended what would have been my isolation. I no longer faced the overwhelming task of finding safe harbor in a university; I now had a group of blockers who ran interference for me. I didn't have to ask girls for dates in the traditional ways of the times. High school girls (whose parents allowed it) were always sprinkled in amongst the mixers and parties so were the pledges from sororities. Truth be told, they were looking for upper classmen, but chemistry is a funny thing—mix enough alcohol with enough hormones and people looked better, sounded smarter, or were too soused to be inhibited. The parties were not of the sort we heard about on television during the Kavanaugh hearings. Raunchy they could be, but at least in our house, you didn't do what someone else didn't want you to do—in part because the odds were there was someone else around who would do it, regardless of what the "it" was.

Worn with pride.

Sober? Unlikely.

Hail! Hail!

ALPHA EPSILON PI

Like he said, 50% of what you learn is not in the classroom.

Our house had a basement, which is where the band set up and the bar was. It didn't much matter where the band set up because the music permeated every nook and cranny of all four floors as loudly as if it was in the next room. There were many multiples of kegs of beer. On non-party nights, there was a juke box on which I played Dean Martin's "Houston" so many times someone removed it from the machine. The basement had one other big room. It held the furnace. The room reeked of oil and had this almost invisible film lining the walls, ceiling, and floor. It's amazing what people will put up with when hormones are in play. Between the band and the furnace, "eau de sweat" was the normal smell downstairs so people naturally gravitated upstairs where there was a large living room. The steps outside that led inside were there as was the kitchen. I know the kitchen had to be inspected by the health department, but still it seemed to have had the same film enveloping it as did the furnace room. Again, during parties it amazed me what people would put up with. The two floors had bedrooms. Enough said there.

What did fraternities do? Well, on St. Patrick's Day, one fraternity dyed dozens of mice green, put them into boxes, took them to the cafeteria and let them go during lunch. More of that later.

One fraternity had a "no more virgins" night and claimed to have hired a hooker. All the pledges who were stupid enough, drunk enough, or both lined up down the hall. If you were first or even second that had some appeal. The guys who were 6,7, or 8th . . . not so much. The first guy looked like he would die of anticipation and anxiety before the clock struck nine, the inviolable starting time. The door opened and in he went. In about four minutes there was a shriek. He burst through the door preceded by a naval ship's worth of curse words. The girl was a guy in drag.

Ah, fraternity life. Another advantage was one person could buy one copy of *The Happy Hooker* and everyone in the house got to read it. Those who read it late in the game found pages that were stuck together . . . well enough of that.

Yes, we had intramural teams. One of our brothers had a black belt in ju-jitsu and taught classes.

We had as mentioned a record of having the highest GPI on campus, so there were mandatory study sessions.

Those who knew the city helped those of us who didn't find good places to take a date. I had a crush of great weight on someone and wanted the most romantic place possible to dine. I ended up by referral in a Hungarian restaurant, low lights, and strolling violinists who came to the table and made one's lady feel like the queen of Hungary. My shirt puffed out so far, I almost burned the buttons off it on the romantic candles set at the table's middle. At seventeen, I thought I'd died and gone to heaven.

The guys with cars drove those who didn't have wheels to various places even home on vacation if they lived near one another. We went to football and basketball games together where being a jerk was encouraged. And there were even times when one's "big brother" became one, someone who would either just listen to the woes of a freshman or who would actively guide one through life's landmines that they likely had either stepped on before or knew someone who did.

And we had an annual awards banquet. Family was invited. Dates dressed like ladies. And we got to prove that maybe the money being spent on us was paying off.

For all of this and more I still send an annual (small) contribution to help support the fraternity.

How sweet it was!

You can figure this out yourself.

Hey, Pledge,

In those days, fraternity and ethnicity or religion went hand in hand. You knew by the fraternity that it would pledge Catholics, Protestants or Jews. At GW, I had two choices: AE Pi (Alpha Epsilon Pi) and TEP (Tau Epsilon Phi). One or two of the others whispered to me, "We wish . . ." I pledged AE Pi because it had two strong selling points. It had the highest GPA of any fraternity on campus and several of its brothers were very "BMOC's," very big men on campus.

Long before it became an issue, GW had banned hazing. Don't get me wrong, being a pledge could be a royal pain in the ass, but it never got you hurt, and it never got you killed. Yes, you could be called at 3 a.m. to pick up a brother's dirty laundry and see to its laundering. Yes, you could be stopped anywhere by a brother and made to follow ridiculous orders—some for lunch, some not eatable or even repeatable. Yes, you had to recite the Greek alphabet at anytime, anywhere and do chores in the house if you blew it. It was mostly Mickey Mouse stuff.

For this you got privileges. You got to sit on the fraternity house steps with older guys and watch the girls walk by and feel like more than you were. You got to hang around in the house which turned the largeness of a university into a neighborhood experience. You got to study with people who had learned how and were determined not to let you be the reason the fraternity would lose its vaunted academic status. You got to go to famous restaurants owned by your president's father and be treated like you were some big shot as people waiting online watched angrily as you were ushered ahead of them to a table. And you got to go to parties—a lot of parties and an occasional fight (see "Food Fight". How's that for foreshadowing?).

Parties

A toga was like a kilt, no one knew what was underneath it—everyone loves a good mystery.

We might as well start with parties because after all isn't that really what fraternities were all about? There were several types. One was a match party with another sorority, sometimes even a non-Jewish house. These were interesting because there was an air of "if my mother knew" pervading both sets of participants and an air of "since I'm never gonna do this again . . ." There were theme parties that were open to anyone so long as they dressed the part. We were famous for our annual toga party. Can you guess why? Here, let me help:

- It was a cheap costume and easy to make. You pulled the top sheet off your bed, twirled around in it, and you were done.
- As easy as it was to put on was as easy as it was to take off.
- Like a kilt, no one knew if there were underpants underneath it.

Another open party was a keg party, though sometimes these were only for brothers, pledges and dates and sometimes held with another sorority. It was an odd thing to name a party because every party in college is a keg party. Go know.

We had two semi-formals, the pledge induction party, and the annual fraternity ball.

About once a quarter we just hired a band and had a nameless party. We used the same band all the time. My freshman year their big numbers were Buddy Holly numbers mixed in with Roy Orbison covers. I loved them both. The next year they showed up in Beatles wigs and my music was swept out the door.

You who are amongst the uninitiated are undoubtably wondering, *So what's the big deal?* It's hard to describe. It wasn't the whole notes or quarters notes in C major, it was the eighth notes and sixteenth notes, in sharps, flats, minor chords. In other words, it was what was between the notes and lines. Unless you came with a date, there was this hormonal electricity of competition for the prettiest girls or the ones rumored to have bad reputations. There was this rule, a brother got first pickin's even if it meant cutting a pledge out who had already begun an interaction with someone.

There was this tug of magnetism. There were only so many places in the house to hide with someone, one was under the furnace in the basement. Unless you didn't care and were happy to do whatever you could get away with there was the couch in the living room, which one year gave the crabs to everyone who used it. Some had no qualms about using hallways or a vacant stretch of wall, or just standing upright or laying out on the carpet hoping at once that no one looked down at you or that they did look down so as not to step on you. A good night was pairing off quickly with someone who was willing and getting to a private place before anyone, or too many anyone's had been drawn to it by the magic magnet of hormones. Under the furnace was prime territory.

At the big parties, the semi-formals, sometimes with real bands in suits and ties, there were no kegs, and everyone behaved like they were at a bar mitzvah, until of course it was over.

I wish I could make it more exciting but understand it this way—I am seventeen and clueless. My mother had been known not to let certain girls into our house even if they had an invitation from me. Here I was now with no rules, any choice of pairing I wanted, and a whole bunch of either more experienced pledges or upper classmen. It was like dance class. You followed the lead until you could take the lead. It is why animals (draw your own references) are more comfortable in herds. AE Pi was my herd.

Some of our pledges and brothers commuted to school from Baltimore or were in residence but whose families lived in Baltimore. Eventually, someone would say to a non-Baltimoran, "ever been to the Gaiety?" A new chapter in out of classroom learning was about to open. It was called the strip club, and of all the strip clubs in all the cities the Gaiety, on Baltimore's notorious "block," was known across the land. And known for one person. Her name was Blaze Starr.

The one and only.

The Block

*We were flirting, tipping . . . maintaining
the attention of the Asian beauty.*

Every major city had one, an area where smut is concentrated. There you find the adult bookstores, go-go clubs, hookers, and strip clubs. Understand my arrival in college brought with me very few exposures to breasts that weren't in *Playboy* magazine. One was when my mother woke up, thought the house was empty and walked out of her bedroom with her slip not completely pulled up. I was about to knock on her door when it opened so we were nose to breast. Scream. Grab at slip. Slam the door. Erotic it wasn't. Then there was the occasional hook up, mostly with lights out. Never had I seen a pair of real mammary glands no less spotlighted and in motion. Never, until I was taken to the block.

In the clubs of the '60s, those that remained anyway, you got the last vestiges of Vaudeville. Often there was an opening act of awful singers or dancers or both. Then there was the comedian. He usually was very funny, corny, dirty, but funny. Then came "the show." There were girls who danced as a build-up and then there was the star. In this case, Blaze Starr. Not only was Blaze Starr the mistress of the former governor of Louisiana, she was a talented, professional stripper, and when she got down to nothing, she looked spectacular as if she were half her age. Today, you can see more of a woman, and sometimes a man, on television than you really saw live and in person on stage. That's why most remaining strip clubs are basically modified whore houses where women give friction dances fully nude in back rooms where other activities can be arranged for negotiated sums of money.

At the go-go clubs, the girls were pretty, fully, if scantily, clothed, and after their set would find a mark, sit at the table and try to get themselves splits of champagne or at least a mixed drink for an outrageous sum of money. At one club, there was this amazing Asian girl. A fraternity brother of mine who was so strong he could lift up the side of a building if he wanted to extract something from the basement was my companion. He was tall, broad-shouldered, from Birmingham, AL, and sounded like it. He reminded me of the coal mine character in the song, "Big Bad John," which was his name. One night at a party, I ran into the girl he was dating, and he was nowhere to be found. She and I were both high and got into a heavy flirt. The next thing I knew, I was rising up the living room wall and it wasn't from alcohol. I felt like a picture about to be hung. After he let me down, he smiled and said, "I guess you forgot. Toby and me—we're a thing." Remember Ralph Kramden? I responded, "Humahumahama . . ." And disappeared.

Back to the go-go club. We were flirting, tipping, and otherwise maintaining the attention of this Asian beauty. As her set ended, he said to me, "Let me show you how this is done." She came over and before she said anything, he ordered her champagne. Another girl joined us. She was cute as a button and had a stomach you could bounce quarters off of. He moved on his quarry with speed and stealth while I, on the other hand sat, again Ralph Kramden-like, trying to make my mouth work. It was pretty intense, but then, sort of suddenly he said, "Time to go." I didn't know why we were abandoning his quest, but I felt a touch of satisfaction that he had failed. He had not shown me how it was done. Night falls along with the curtain on this act.

It rises in the morning. I was in the juke box room in the basement looking to see if the brothers had made good on their pledge that they were going to destroy the copy of Dean Martin's singing of "Houston," which for some reason mesmerized me and I would play sometimes a dozen times in a row. Hence the threat. I find it, sighed a sigh of relief, and exited into the hallway. Also exiting into that hallway from the furnace room were John and Miss Asian Go-Go Get'em. She looked mussed and well worn. She was missing her stage presence and costume. John on the other hand looked like the cat that had just eaten the canary. No inferences otherwise meant. He winked at me later telling me that we left the club with her phone number in his hand. He picked her up at the end of her shift, 1 a.m., and had been adding heat to the furnace all night. He had showed me how it was done.

Let me add this. John paid for four years of college at the poker table. You never bet against him. He just didn't lose.

"Venezuelans live on 3 dollars a month. That's a tragedy. That is impossible to survive under these conditions."

– Juan Guido, politician, activist, former president Venezuelan National Assembly, studies in International Affairs and did post-graduate work in Political Management

Lorelai

She was a beauty. She was about 5'2" tall, with long, honey brown hair . . . a smile that could be weaponized.

This is a year out of order, but it serves as a non-Greek story. I believe it was my sophomore year. The dorm known as "super-dorm" was finished. "Super" because all the other dorms were vintage small apartment buildings. This was new construction, taller than most, held probably three times the number of students and . . . it was the first co-ed dorm at GW, maybe in the country.

It is my understanding that today co-ed dorms mean one's neighbor could be of either sex or, if not, there isn't much restricting one from going from one floor to another. Super dorm had alternating floors by sex and an interior design created by engineers that were supposed to create a student's nightmare to get from one floor to the next. What was the nightmare was not for the students, it was for the dorm managers. It didn't take too long before boys and girls ended up on each other's floors, the overwhelming number of them not studying engineering. Theoretically, once you took a hallway exit, you ended up either at the locked door of the roof or the open door of the lobby. How the elevators figured out what you were, I don't remember. Maybe key cards.

Now a vaunted, upper classman, on arrival day, I was one of a large school of male sharks swimming in circles in the lobby of the dorm. We were there to help. Right. If you believe that, I'll show you my list of bridges for sale. We were there to scope out the schools of new female fish. It is hard to distinguish quality amidst a crush of quantity, but sometimes God is good. As I scanned the waters, I saw a family trying to get the attention of the registration staff, all of whom looked like they wished the kids had gone to trade school or gotten sick that day. Harried comes close to how they looked and try as they might, they couldn't work fast enough to make the pool of anxious parents less deep in front of them. I saw this tall man, his wife, and a daughter that was hard to describe beyond the word "perfect." It turns out she wasn't, but that's for later.

She was adorable; winsome or wholesome also work. She was a beauty. She was about 5'3" tall, with long, honey brown hair, a smile that could be weaponized, and as I got closer, a figure that was neither model-thin nor athlete hard. She took my breath away.

God decided to have a good time. I worked my way over to them, made an introduction, and asked if I could be of some help. I was received like the returning Jesus, and yes, it so happened I could be of help. I knew one of the desk girls in heart-attack mode, got her to take care of the family, and found whilst that was happening, I could share some "impress the family time." It turned out that daddy was a dentist, as was mine. They, too, were from New York, though the "Island," not Brooklyn. In mere minutes, I was part of the family. "Helpers" were that day allowed on any floor, so I offered to help and got them up to her room all the while trying to find a spot I could disappear into and stay for the semester. Just kidding, just kidding. Actually not.

I did ask her name, and I must confess, without a yearbook, some fifty years later, I have no idea what it was. When her folks were leaving, I also asked if I could show her around and then buy her a bite to eat. The answers were soon and yes. So, I bid my farewells and left with a time and place to meet. For the next few days, I felt I had become addicted, or that if I had died, I'd gone to heaven. If this was to be my one and only romantic encounter, I felt life couldn't get better. But it wasn't to be.

As fraternity week began, so did the excuses. I said she wasn't perfect, and she wasn't. First of all, she wasn't Jewish. That meant she would soon be running with a different crowd to different fraternity and sorority parties. She also had the same effect on about 300 other guys as she did on me, many of them juniors or seniors trumping my now lowly, sophomore status. We saw each other a lot given the compact nature of the campus, but I could only get so close, only get a smile, which was like getting a sniff of coke to a drug addict, only see that long hair which swept down over one eye, Veronica-like, then swing over her shoulder as she turned and went in another direction. Within weeks she had a beau at the Sigma Chi house, a fraternity whose crest featured a cross. Worse yet, it was three or four doors down from my fraternity, AE Pi, so she was never out of sight for long, either coming or going.

Of those college credit courses I took in high school, one course I took was in Greek Mythology, which I loved. I remember the story of the Sirens, the diaphanous women who populated the rocks and sang to the sailors, sailors who had been at sea for months. The experienced captains knew to have their crews fill their ears with wax and cover their eyes to avoid the sounds and sights of the Sirens. Some were even lashed to the masts—early Tokyo Rose, I guess.

But alas, loneliness (read horniness), and the tales of the great beauty and comfort offered by the Sirens was overpowering even before the ships got to them. And as the myth goes, many a ship veered off course with everyone who could find a spyglass leaning over the sides searching desperately for the Sirens and paying no attention to the boats, which ended up dashing themselves to pieces, with the entranced men sent to Davey Jones' Locker. For their lives, they found not even a mermaid as they went down. The Sirens had bewitched them out of their lives.

Oh yes, the queen of the Sirens was named Lorelai.

FOOD FIGHT—
The Real One

*The pledges were supposed to cut the pies
and serve their big brothers.*

If boys will be boys, then fraternity boys will be more so. Why what took place was easy to figure out. Picture two bull moose (mease?) (meases?), a youngster and the established herd's leader, circling themselves for weeks snorting, stomping, making intimidating rushes at one another. Those would be me, the master of the fraternity, and a pledge who himself came from money and was in no time dating the daughter whose dad owned a well-known, car rental company. He was a transfer to GW from another school's football team, a tight end if I remember. Except from quarterbacks, he was not one to take orders, from the master or not. The master was widely acknowledged to be one of the biggest of the big men on campus and also came from powerful, monied stock. One day there was bound to be a clash of antlers.

Where it happened was the surprise. A pledge-brother night out had been called to begin with dinner at the venerable Maryland deli, Hofberg's. We had a table for many, a big rectangle, fortunately as it turns out, away from the rest of the patrons. Brothers were sitting with their pledges and of course there was a lot of trash-talk going on amongst mouths filled with sour pickles, corned beef, and knishes. The Master of the fraternity, a demi-God both in the fraternity and the university in part because of his varied talents, shall we say, and in part because his dad owned a restaurant that was "the place to be" in DC for business and political deals, sat at the head of the table. Just his last name struck fear into many—but not into his "little brother" who actually was bigger than he.

Let me give you one example. This was in his senior year. There was on campus an exquisite Greek goddess who was a sophomore. One day, she passed by the fraternity house while all of us were on the front steps having a college "learn-in" at the knee of the Master. He took one look at her and said, "I will have her." We scoffed. He didn't even know her name. One of the brothers said how will we know if you do? His response: (remember this is the '60s and at a fraternity house) "I'll bring you her underpants."

And one late night he did. The man-boys who were there were insane with awe and jealously. The rumor of conquest spread like wildfire. His God-like status was confirmed. I, however, of the logical mind, didn't buy it. Leaders don't have to always do what it has been said they've done. They only have to have people believe they did it. My guess? He took her to dad's restaurant, wined and dined her, snowed her with Washington insider stories and then probably said, "Hey, wanna help me pull a fast one on my fraternity? She, now several sheets to the wind, thinks, "I can play with the boys," totters off to the girl's room, drops her draws, steals a napkin for wrapping and "Voila!" Decades later, I found out I was right.

This is the first time a word of this has come out of my mouth, or in this case my keyboard and only because of the demise of our leader. He didn't even make it to his '70s.

Now to his pledge.

This Long Islander, with red hair and a mashed nose, had a body that had "linebacker" written all over it, though he was a tight end. He boded well for the fraternity's intra-mural football fortunes. He also was "dating well." He was creating his own legends—and myths.

Came time for dessert. The consensus was lemon merengue pie. Several were ordered. The pledges were supposed to cut the pies and serve their big brothers. Quick as a wink, Mr. Mashed Nose swooped up a whole pie in his shovel size paws and like on the Milton Berle show when someone yelled, "MAAAAKE UP!" and Berle got a powder puff in the face, our Master was suddenly, so suddenly he didn't even flinch, dripping lemon meringue. That was the beginning. Food began flying everywhere.

The end of what began a two-act play was the also sudden realization of what we had done to the restaurant. Like roaches when the lights are turned on, we all scattered out any door that would open.

I don't know who paid the bill. In fact, as we scattered, we heard sirens in the distance. We pledges spilled out of the restaurant and launched ourselves into cars. As we were headed back to the house, I did not know that this Keystone Cops chase to the fraternity house was the beginning of act two—the capture and defense against the brothers by the pledges of the fraternity house where many of the brothers lived.

Keep reading.

With what does one use to defend a four-story house that is legal and not lethal? It also had to be handy because the brothers were hot on our trail. Soon we would be surrounded. The answer? Water balloons of which we had plenty—balloons and water. Why we had hundreds of balloons I haven't a clue; we just did. Must have been from a party past or a party future.

Soon real leadership was shown. One pledge became Odysseus marking up the defense against whomever Odysseus was defending against. This group fetched the balloons. That group filled them to breaking. Another group opened all the windows and locked all the doors. A sentry was posted while other pledges were scattered amongst the open windows and the roof. Wastepaper baskets, garbage cans, and any available receptacles were filled with the super-charged balloons and distributed like ammunition at the

Alamo to the defenders. Those not filled with balloons were filled with water, 5, 10, 15, 25 gallons of it along with whatever happened to be in the container before it got shanghaied. "Bring it on!" We were ready.

Within minutes the sentry shouted an alert. Brothers began piling out of cars that came at the house from both sides, which was in the middle of G Street's buildings, even though it was a one-way street. Swerving and screeching, cars came to a halt in any and all directions. As the brothers began yelling threats, looking up and thus raising their faces to the windows to do so, it began to rain water bombs. A water bomb was a three-pronged weapon. First and most obvious was the water. It drenched the target to the bone. The second was the shock of being hit by this two- or three-pound weapon. The third was the snap against one's skin as the balloon burst. The sky was filled with them, raining down on the unprepared, unprotected, and very unhappy brothers. The tide, so to speak, was running with us. Then it turned. After all, it was just water.

Act two: The tide turns. Our upper-class brothers, the ones responsible for the house having the highest GPI of any house on campus, these leaders that we were to follow through the academic jungles and come out better than we went in, these upper-class brothers finally realized that the front door was unlocked. As the one genius who opened the flood gates called to the others, a rush of angry, revenge-seeking, fraternity men charged up the stairs towards the front door.

We wet-behind-the-ears freshmen, however, were ready. We retreated to the second floor, the only access to which was a narrow staircase. A cyclone of water met those on their way up and drove them back down. Meantime, the third floor was reloading and the troops on the roof were whomping the slow poke brothers with bomb after bomb, can after can. Sheets of water poured out of the sky onto the street. The street looked like a street cleaning truck had exploded in front of the house. We were losing ground, but we were becoming legends. Legends attract attention. Hence act three.

Act Three: As explained, the university is in a unique place. It is two blocks from the White House and the Executive Office building (then the office of the vice-president). It was about six blocks from the State Department and one more to the Washington Monument. About a five-minute walk brought you to the Lincoln Memorial. Checkered around this space were things like the World Health Organization and the World Bank not to mention the university itself. What that meant was that at any given moment, it was possible to rally police officers from the District of Columbia, the University, the Secret Service, Park Police, the State Department PD, and as back up from across the river the United States Army from Fort Myer. Keep that in mind, as did we when at first, far in the distance, sirens began to penetrate our heads.

The District is small and at night traffic is sparse. We didn't have much time. Suddenly, the combatants were brothers in arms. We scattered. Everyone knew a sure-fire hiding place, but it had to be close because in minutes the streets would look like a red-light convention. So many cop car lights were spinning, to look at them was almost a psychedelic experience. Many of these cops had bull horns, they all had guns, and none of them looked at all happy having to step out of their dry cars into Lake G. Street.

For a moment, I froze. I'd like to think I was thinking. As wet as I was, I could have been making in my pants and not known it. Then something snapped. A light went off in my head, fortunately not creating a blown fuse from water induced short-circuiting. I could see the headline, "STUDENT GETS CHARRED STANDING IN THE STREET." The furnace room! As everyone scattered like rats leaving a sinking ship, most running into the arms of uniformed people, I ran downstairs, to the back of the house, seeking out that oily smelling safe haven. Like an infantry man in battle, I hit the floor and scooched myself towards the big, black, cast iron savior pushing dust bunnies and prophylactics out of the way. Without much thought, born of not having much time (the stomping sounds of the pursuing police engulfed the house. The yelling and cursing were deafening), I slithered far under the huge monster only later thinking that if it went on, I was probably not in a very good place after all. Poached Gralnick.

Act Four: The Finale. I spent the night under the furnace, which did not go on and under which no one bothered to look. Scores of brothers and pledges were tossed into cop cars and taken I don't know where. I do know after a few hours of stewing in fear, long distance calls to parents, the dean of men figured enough was enough. He gathered our fraternity officers in his office, read them the riot act, and put the house on probation.

To this day, show me someone in a restaurant carrying a piece of lemon meringue pie and I can feel my "flight and fight" mechanisms begin to rev up, my eyes begin to dart around for escape routes, beads of sweat breaking out on my forehead, and police sirens begin to whine in my ears. I order cherry pie.

*"Live every day like it's your last
because one day you'll be right."*

– Jerry Reinsdorf, tax attorney
with IRS, billionaire mega
sports owner in Chicago,
graduated in 1957

The embarrassment still lingers . . .

Sloshed

Getting drunk, wasted, sloshed, wall-eyed was near the top of most everyone's to-do list.

Especially for kids like me, part of what college held out as excitement was getting drunk. I had a thing with alcohol. I didn't drink much, or much like it. My mom was an alcoholic and I'm sure that had a lot to do with it. Yet, getting drunk, wasted, sloshed, wall-eyed was near the top of every freshmen's to-do list, and with a week of orientation there was plenty of time to at least dip one's toes into the ocean of the devil's brew, so to speak, that awaited us. And I did.

Let me start by saying I heard that someone died of alcohol poisoning freshman year. It was at a football game. He had a bottle of vodka. Someone dared him to chug it. As they say, "Some mistakes you don't get to make twice." So, unlike some of my classmates who began to live by the bottle and then die, I was more measured.

For instance, after a round of fraternity parties orientation week, I found I had downed more beer in a few hours than I had in the previous year. And the previous year, while still home and in high school, that certainly wasn't a lot. In the drunken state, one sees oneself differently. In fact, normally one doesn't see oneself at all.

Drunk you notice that you are talking but sometimes it's to no one, that you are weaving like a loom trying to get down the sidewalk to someplace, you think you are walking arrow straight. Eventually, what you do notice is that you've never had to go to the bathroom so badly in your life. Then you begin to do stupid student tricks.

As mentioned before, I had this "double thing" going on for a while. First, I did an uncanny imitation of Snoopy imitating the vulture. One night a pack of us were wandering around Foggy Bottom/Adams Morgan and we came to the Capital Hilton. It is almost spitting distance from Lafayette Park and the White House. In front of the hotel, which is done in one of those styles called Classic, were two large rectangular ledges flanking the entrance. They seemed to say to my slightly inebriated brain, *we are in need of a bird to perch here.* Buzzards there were aplenty circling the skies, I assume alerting those far and near that yet another politician would soon be available as political kill, but I was closer. With a little help from my friends, I scrambled to my perch and spent about fifteen minutes being part of whatever the classic design was. Most interesting was that the people on the street, the people entering and exiting the hotel, even the doorman, all took me in stride. I guess it was sort of "after you've seen presidents, and spies, and generals what's to get excited about a kid who thinks he's a vulture?" So, for the next two years, never did we pass the hotel that I wasn't urged by my crew to do my thing, and I did even sober.

Junior year, I lost my pin feathers and grew up.

The low light of this phase of life took place at the Lincoln Memorial. It was a painfully, cold, winter night, and we were warming ourselves with liquor, beer, and women at our apartment. Since this was my junior year, you can see how many pin feathers I'd actually lost and how grown up I'd really become. Wrong. There was tension in the house the kind caused by several drinking males all having eyes for the same girl. I was one of them and since I had convinced myself she was there for me, I was mightily irritated when someone else made the successful move on her. With a very audible "Harumph!" and some sprinkled expletives, I announced I was going for a walk. Without too much detail, one of the other girls said, "Hey! (or Hey, schmuck) it's cold outside." In my best John Wayne, I grumbled, "I'll be fine. Don't worry about me." With that everyone took me at my word and the worrying passed quickly. I headed down the stairs and out the door, which of course, I slammed behind me. In about four travelled feet, it dawned on me, "Shit. It's cold out here." John Wayne would not have gone back and said, "Excuse me, Mary, but I forgot my scarf." Neither did I. The problem was that I had forgotten more than my scarf.

It had been chokingly hot in the apartment; we were dressed (some mostly not) accordingly. Once outside, I realized I was not wearing shoes, just sweat socks; I was not wearing a jacket, or a shirt, but a v-neck undershirt, and over my underpants I had on a pair of shorts. In other words, had I gone back in, I would have had to come out with a wardrobe of winter clothes. I did however have the foresight to take a pint of rum. It was a pretty straight shot from my apartment door to the Lincoln Memorial. A straight but none too short a shot. I couldn't get lost, but I could get frostbite. By the time it was in sight, I had no feeling in my entire body, I couldn't walk a curved line no less a straight one, but what I did begin to feel was not well.

As I approached the shrubbery around the side of this mammoth structure, I heard voices. It was the constabulary. I was sober enough to know this was not a good place to be at that hour, dressed like I was dressed, and drunk as I was. Then too, this growing sense of very unwellness was overtaking me. As the voices approached, I dove, maybe tilted and fell, into the hedges. I pulled myself behind them having now the cold marble pressing on my back, and the leafless twigs poking my face. Somehow, they missed me and continued about their appointed rounds. Maybe two minutes later, I became the first person I had ever heard of who had thrown up so to speak at the feet of our sixteenth president.

I have no memory of how I got back home. I do remember the

remaining partiers looking at me oddly as I made my way to my room.

I also remember being deathly ill for about two weeks.

Next morning, everything hurt. I couldn't even put clothing next to my skin. My roommate, white as Protestants come, was in the kitchen frying up spam and slopping mayonnaise on it. I couldn't decide if I should cut my wrists, my throat or his. It's called alcohol poisoning. I managed to pull myself together that Sunday morning, wishing I had the fortitude and memory to pray. I went to the pharmacy. The pharmacist didn't say word. He reached for that aforementioned bottle of Vitamin B6 (I think) and then said, "two every four hours and don't drink anything stronger than water—for about a week."

I didn't.

PS:

If walking drunk (and half naked) is a bad idea, driving drunk is a far worse one. You don't know how much worse until you've done it, assuming you survived to remember what it was like. I did. The first tip, back then, that you maybe shouldn't be driving, is that you can't quite get the key into the door lock and then again into the ignition. It almost but not quite makes it. It misses slightly to the left or right or both, above and below until you steady your first hand with the second and ram it in. "That wasn't so bad," your brain, or the devil whispers. The next thing you don't notice is that usually you slide into the seat; this time you hit it like you'd fallen off the roof of a building and gone through the roof of your car, unless it was a convertible that was open, and hit the seat with the force of a pod of bricks. Now there you are, seated, hands on the wheels, engine ignited and purring. "Everything seems jake here," says your brain or the devil.

Pulling out of the parking space you probably hear a little click, the sound of your fender not quite clearing the fender of the car in front. "I hardly heard that, how bad could it be?" says your brain— or the devil. Out into traffic you pull and you're on your way. There's traffic, nothing is moving much more than twenty-five mph, there are cars in front and on both sides of you. Hemmed in, the car seems to be on the straight and narrow so you as the pilot feel in control. Finally, you see the highway sign. It says 295 but you see 229955.

Traffic has thinned out, speeded up, and you realize that since you were last out on this road that the white lines had loosened from the pavement, probably from the summer's heat, your brain or the devil tells you. They don't quite seem to be anchored to anything. The road has a slight wave to it, like watching a calm sea from the shore. Both the lines and the lanes are moving so nothing makes more sense than to move with them. This is known as weaving. One of the problems of weaving, even without an on-looking Officer of the Law, is that if you are in the lane closest to on-coming traffic, you can weave yourself right into the front of a car coming at you around sixty mph. No voice gives you this piece of arithmetic awareness. The force of two 2000 lb cars going sixty miles an hour is 4000 lbs x 120 mph. The answer to the equation is not a number; it is a word—death. But now, when you could use a little coaching, the brain and the devil have gone to the men's room. On you go.

We're out in the country now. The moon beams are slipping through the branches, some with leaves and some not. This gives the impression that wind or not, the branches are moving, like arms with long swirling, red fingers reaching out to snatch you from your car. You roll (yes roll) and put your hand on a handle and move it in circular motions until the window rises from the door and seals itself into the roof. Things—deer? Reflections? Nothing?—like carnival pieces seem to pop up from the highway. Naturally, you use your best driver's training reflexes to avoid them. This is called swerving. It often ends up with you and your car in a heap on the side of the road soon bathed in the swirling red light of a highway patrol car the officer from which is asking you sensible questions to which you are answering in non-sensible sentences. Sometimes, you realize how silly you sound, and you begin to giggle. That is a bad and costly thing to do. What happens next is this cop, just to trick you, picks one of the white lines that got loose from the pavement and tells you to walk a straight line on it. "C'mon! Really?" Your brain or the devil says, "One of The Flying Wallendas couldn't walk on this thing."

The result of this snappy repartee ends with the cops handcuffing you. They call the dean of men. The dean of men calls your parents. Both of them have to be dealt with while hung over. You get hell from both. The state divests hundreds of dollars from you and your license for a while. The Dean threatens you with expulsion which you know doesn't come with a refund for the semester. And your parents take away either your car or your privilege to drive anyone else's car. Meanwhile, the devil is laughing his—or her—ass off.

Thank God that never happened to me.

You sell what?!?

It was an explanation he had given many times—pornography.

Let us remember, I arrived at college a wet-behind-the-ears, seventeen-year-old virgin whose mother beat the hell out of him upon discovering his he thought well-hidden, sole copy of a *Playboy* magazine. So, I had, as a freshman, lots to learn beyond what I would learn in the classes for which I had registered. The fraternity provided a lot of it and sometimes that was just random invites to random parties not held at school. This is such a one.

One night, I found myself with a group of friends at a get together at one of their houses. We were in northern Virginia. The intent was good. The parents wanted to do a favor for us newbies and had invited us to a barbecue. Since the Health Department had closed the student cafeteria for a time any trustworthy source of food was welcome. We chatted, drank beer, and were having an evening that could have been a Norman Rockwell look at any backyard in America. That was until I sidled up to a conversation some guys I knew were having with a guy I didn't. He wouldn't have spoiled Mr. Rockwell's picture. He was wearing as I recall chinos, dark shoes, a white shirt with a tie, and jacket thrown over a chair. That was a conversation starter or interrupter. "Why are you all duded up?" I asked. He replied that he had to go to work after the party but was in no hurry. He had plenty of time.

Really, what do you do? He replied in a very straight forward manner, one that matched his dress code. It was an explanation he had given many times. "You know how newspapers are dropped off to stores at odd hours by their vendors? I do something like that with magazines."

"No foolin'," I said, a nice Jewish boy to this nice Jewish boy, "what kind of magazines?"

"Pornography."

That's all he said, "Pornography." I said, "No shit!" Then it began to get interesting. Since his drops were after 1 a.m. he did have plenty of time to take us back to school from the party and there was plenty of time yet before we had to leave. That meant maybe I had time to do some drying behind my wet ears, assuming I could get into his trunk and lift part of the "stash."

He had another idea. He used that plenty of time to get plowed. I'm sure we pre-college students were told by our parents about taking people's keys or calling cabs. "Don't ever get in a car with an impaired driver!" Maybe we weren't told soon enough or maybe we were a little too skunked to be thinking clearly or maybe we were hoping that instead of in the trunk, the porno mags would be strewn around the seats of the car. Thus, advice thrown to the winds, the appointed hour came, and we took off with the budding Hugh Hefner at the wheel—took off almost literally. Took off as in like a rocket. As we hit the beltway in his Super 88, I noticed that our speed was increasing to speedway numbers. We weren't on the speedway or even the highway yet. We flew past eighty and left ninety behind. Soon, we were leaving behind all the other cars on the road. Had he been sober enough to read the traffic signs, he couldn't have anyway because they were going by too fast. "Where's a cop when you need one?" Panic inched upward within me along with the speedometer. In those days, speedometers had speeds on them that only racing cars have now. His showed 120 mph and once we did make the highway, it wasn't long before the needle was pressed flat against that number begging for the addition of a 130 or 140.

The thing one has to remember about a beltway is that it is designed to go around a city. It is a circle, or as our chauffer decided, a racetrack. Round and round she goes, where she stops no one knows. Going 120 mph, it doesn't take long to zip through Virginia, come around into Maryland, and end up once again in Virginia. Three, four, maybe five times.

Though blurred, things were beginning to look familiar. It was like being on a runaway merry-go-round. It was terrifying. Fortunately, an 8-cylinder car going 120 miles per hour gets about three miles to the gallon. Finally, we began to run out of gas. We pulled off at an exit onto a county road and were three lights from a gas station. The first light was red. God was on our side. We were stationary and next to another car. As we considered jumping him, next to us pulled up a more welcome sight. It was a state trooper. Like someone had lighted our pants on fire, we all leaped out of the car. Along with our pants, we were acting like our hair was on fire. That was enough to attract his attention. Obviously used to drunk college age kids, he slowly emerged from his cruiser and asked Hugh for his license and registration. In us he had no interest. The magazines would definitely be late this night.

By the way, there was no porno in the back seat. Maybe given the circumstances that was a good thing.

Oddest of all, I have no recollection of how we got home.

Ben?

IF IT'S

St. Paddy's Day...

*Sometimes there is a trigger that . . . makes
the dumb seem comprehensible.*

It was a prank, and it wasn't born of my fraternity. Also, it wasn't the reason the health department closed the cafeteria, but it could have been. Once one is in school for a month or so, a routine sets in. You begin to feel like you've been there forever or will be. Tinges of boredom set in and it isn't long before students are doing dumb things, many of which are described on these pages.

Sometimes, all it takes is something popping into the heads of a group of people. Sometimes they are drunk, and the ideas are those one would expect from a drunk group of teenagers. Sometimes there is a trigger that at least makes the dumb seem comprehensible. And so, it was that first St. Paddy's day in school.

Washington, DC, as we have explored, is built on a swamp and ends at a river. There is therefore no shortage of mice and rats. River rats are not to be messed with. Many are the size of small dogs but without the temperament of small dogs. It was not unusual especially on a rainy night to see to what looked like a gang of rats, dozens in a pack, racing from sewer to sewer their beady red eyes glaring at you as they passed. Bad enough it would be to have been attacked by them, and there was always the possibility of one being rabid. Having had a series of rabies shots as a kid, this was not something I wanted even to entertain again, much less have happen.

If we were to do something with four-legged, disgusting creatures, mice would be the choice. Besides which, one could go to the local pet shop and buy as many as you wanted. Much easier than trying to catch them. Why, you wonder, would someone keep a mouse for a pet? Well, Michael Jackson made a whole movie and hit song about his pet mouse, Ben. As long as you don't have a male and female, they make cute, cuddly pets. If you have a male and female, they make more mice, many more mice. Mice breed at spectacular rates. Then you have to buy a snake to eat the mice, which is pretty disgusting, or let them go which is really not a very nice thing to do to your neighbors.

I know something about mouse multiplication. In high school, I had to do a science experiment. I chose the effect of adrenaline on mice's ability to negotiate a maze they were familiar with. I bought two, cute, little mice, put them in a ten-gallon fish tank, sans ten gallons of water and over the next two weeks "did my thing." It was interesting. More interesting was the Sunday morning I went to check on them and two had become I think ten, the eight new ones being tiny, hairless, pink babies.

I was a bright boy. and I had seen *The Sorcerer's Apprentice*. Why it didn't dawn on me that this happening would happen again and then yet again, I don't know. Now, I had a lot of mice; they needed some *lebensraum*, so I went to the hardware store and bought a wooden, mice homestead for them. My rodent family was well, and I was happy—happy until at some ungodly hour of a Sunday morning my father crashed into my room having a conniption fit. I'd never seen him that color before, or anyone that color before. He dragged me into their bathroom where I saw little mice running all over the place. He put his face into mine and growled, "Get them out of here before your mother wakes up!"

We lived in a three-story house built around 1900. Originally, attached to the furnace there was a metal pipe called a heat-riser that ran up through every floor emitting heat as it went. When radiators came in, the pipes went out, but for some reason in our house they never closed the pipe holes. From the attic you could drop a penny down that hole, and it would end up on the first floor. I had by that time learned a lot about mice. What I didn't learn was that even small rodents have extremely sharp teeth and powerful jaws. I guess like many a wizened prisoner they spent weeks executing their escape plan. They chewed through the wood and wire and took off. I guess there's a little lemming in mice because one went for the heat-riser hole and the rest followed. How they landed on the second floor and not the first I could never figure out, but they did, and there they were about five feet from the foot of my mother's bed. She, normally one who could sleep through an explosion, was peacefully asleep, snoring like a freight-train.

Shift to the bathroom, I am scurrying around the floor with or like the mice. My father is standing over my shoulder. Let me just say this, catching mice is not easy. But mother slept on—until she didn't. She sat up and groggily inquired, "Abe, why is Billy crawling around on the bathroom floor?" Now my dad was not about to let the mice out of the bag. He responded, "It's nothing. Go back to sleep." That didn't happen. The fog cleared, she figured it out, and she let out a *gashrei* (Yiddish for scream but the translation really doesn't do it justice).

There's more but I think I've made the point that I knew something about mice and pandemonium, so on we go.

That March, a group of fraternity boys (not mine) got this idea. They would buy a few dozen mice. Since they weren't keeping them long their sex didn't matter. They proceeded to the supermarket and bought lots and lots of green food dye. In short order they were the proud owners of several dozen Irish mice. Come lunch one day, a group of students are noted walking into the cafeteria carrying shoe boxes. Thinking back, I thought that was odd but, in the moment, with lines snaking in and around the food, people scrambling to tables, and dragging chairs to tables that hadn't enough to accommodate them and their friends, carrying their book bags, the engineering students with their magic rulers, if someone did notice the boxes, they didn't register. And the din of all this was so great they never heard the scratching and squeaking of the boxes' occupants.

Once seated—boys and their mice—the boxes were slid under the table. At a coordinated moment, when the cafeteria seemed more jam-packed than the fire department sign on the wall said was legal, the lids came off and there began a mass prisoner escape. Now remember, mice are little and they were on the floor. It took a while before they were noticed. That happened I believe when one panicked creature created another, this one two-legged, when it ran over her sneaker and started up her leg. "Blood-curdling" would be a good phase to describe the scream that came from her mouth. Within moments, mice and girls were running all over the place. I am not a good enough writer to describe the chaos.

I do remember two things. One was a group of students high-tailing it for the door yelling, "Happy St. Paddy's Day." The other was the realization that went like this: *Why would anyone want to be the Dean of Men?*

CNN's Dana Bash described the chaotic first presidential debate between Donald Trump and Joe Biden as a "s*** show" live on air during the . . .

"If you get the dirty end of the stick, sharpen it and turn it into a useful tool."

– Colin Powell, MBA 1971, BA 1990

"If I did not attend GW, my career would not be what it is today. My professors helped guide and connect me to GW alumni, and being in D.C. meant I was able to intern and get valuable experience while in school as well as the summers. I am forever grateful that I am a Colonial."

– Dana Bash, BA 1993

119

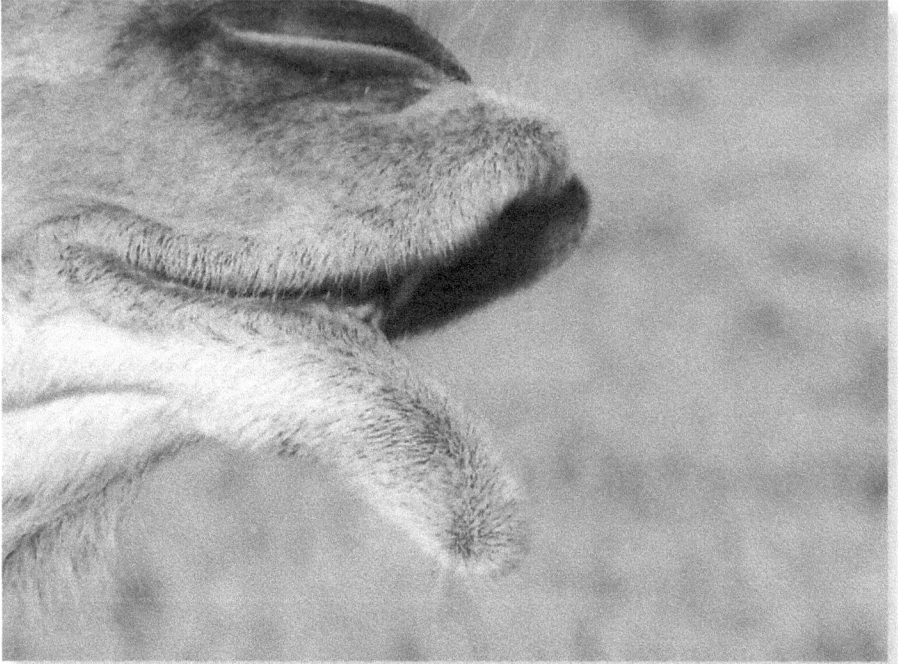

He brayed far better than I.

WOULD YOU BUY A

Used Car

FROM

This Man?

**Did you know you could drive a car for years
without an emergency brake?**

A fair number of freshmen came to school with cars. Since GW had a large commuter population many were cars used just to go from home to school. Others came across state lines with their owners. The school had no rules about first year students and cars like many schools do now. The only problem, like in any city, is where the hell you were putting it when you were not using it. The fraternity house had a driveway, but if you weren't last in and first out, you'd better have hoped that you had no need of the car until about eleven each morning. For me, no car, no problem.

It wasn't until I had moved off campus and had proven I would survive and do well in college that I even brought up the subject. I was home for a visit and we in turn were visiting the family at my Uncle Al's, the man my brother not so affectionately called, "The Baron of High Point," because he owned 247 acres of prime Westchester County land. On it sat his private psychiatric hospital and family residence. My uncle understood wanting cars. Though he drove very little (up the hill from house to hospital and back, sometimes to Brooklyn to see us, sometimes to the city for a conference or a board meeting, and mostly to East Chester (about as far away from Port Chester as it sounds) to see his best friend Eddie, he bought a new Cadillac every year. Both his kids had cars courtesy of my aunt and I had learned to drive on his property when no one was looking. So, he made me a deal.

He would **LEND** me enough money to purchase a small, used car. This had to be, he told me sternly, the first bill I paid every month. If I failed to pay on time, he would close out the loan and take the car. Love is like a prism. Depending on how you look at it, it shows different things to different people. Promise made, I got my car. And I loved it. It was a two-year-old, red, VW convertible. In its own way, it had the caché of a lot of the other cars that were Jaguar XKE's or souped-up, 8-cylinder Olds'. It had a certain *je ne sais quoi* about it. It was also four on the floor. I loved it even though its size and gear shift made it virtually impossible to do what boys dream about doing in cars, unless of course the top was down, and you didn't mind standing up . . . Yes, it was mine and I did love it.

Then came the day the *Herbie the Love Bug* movie came out. Why, we were now Hollywood stars. I took a young lady on the first date the bug was to host. I wanted for us to be able to show off our car stuff. It was a beautiful, Saturday afternoon and we decided to go to the zoo through the famous, at times infamous, Rock Creek Park, an island of wilderness plunked down inside part of DC and part of Virginia.

I was nervous as a cat. My skills as a four on the floor driver were nascent to say the least. The girl was very pretty to say the least. And long before GPS, I had no idea where I was going, to say the least. My focus was not the radio, not her perfume, not the gorgeous scenery. No, it was on making sure I remembered the gear pattern and didn't hit a deer or pedestrian while doing it. Well, into the park and about halfway by estimation to the zoo, my date said something like, "Do you smell something burning?" I snapped to attention. You know, I did. I looked into the rear-view mirror to see this black cloud being laid down behind my car like a WW II destroyer laying down a smoke screen to protect the fleet. My mind flashed to my business deal. What did it say about my obligations were if the car went up in a blaze of fire and smoke? Then it hit me. I hadn't released the emergency brake, which by the time of discovery was in the midst of its own emergency.

Did you know you could drive a car for years without an emergency brake? I didn't, but I did.

The rest of the date doesn't warrant too much more ink but for two things. One is that a camel spit at us. That ranks amongst the five most disgusting things that can ever happen to a person. The other was the monkeys were horny and put on a show other's might have seen as a lesson to be recalled later in the day, but that both my date and I found too embarrassing even to acknowledge and walked silently away.

The car had only one more notable moment in its life, it was courtesy of Warner Bros. (Yes, those guys whose initials [WB] you see in the theaters before cartoons and movies.) That's a good teaser, no?

Jerry Warner was opening a documentary division of his company and he wanted to do a documentary on the nation's capital. As a tourist guide, I was recommended to him. I don't remember if by my brother, then at CBS or my boss at the Heritage Cavaliers Guide Company ("where," the brochure proclaimed, "all the guides were licensed, clean cut, college-aged and in uniform"). We had a preliminary meeting and I recall another. He was interested in what I outlined for him to tell the stories that made the District and its monuments come alive.

He said he would be in touch but wasn't. Months went by. We

come to the dead of winter and the height of an unusual event for Washington, a real by-the-numbers snowstorm. The phone rings. It's Warner. "I'm in Virginia and I need to see you now. When can you be here?" I knew where he was staying, said given the weather it could take an hour. He replied. "Step on it!" and click. Having figured the line was dead, I threw on some clothing and ran downstairs to test for the first time the legend that Herbie and his cousins were wonderful in the snow because their motors were in the back giving them great traction because of the weight on top of the rear wheels. Off I went with "step on it" ringing in my ears and the promise of a multi-thousand dollars payday interrupting my focus.

I swung onto the Memorial Bridge, waving to Abe as we passed. On the Virginia side, the snow had been shoveled but only one lane was open. I approached a large, white curve with a sheen coming from it from the now sunny sky. All the snow that went into making that lane was piled high into a bank that ran for hundreds of yards. I should have known the sheen meant ice; I had depended on Herbie knowing that. He didn't.

We whipped into the curve . . . and kept whipping. The next thing I knew, I was door high surrounded by drift. There I sat. Remember, I said no GPS. Same goes for cell phones. It seemed like hours before a state trooper happened by. He dug out my door. I got out of the car and together we slid the car back onto the road. In those days, Southern "staties" were nice—unless you were a darker color than the snow. So, with a little less speed and a lot more caution, I continued on my way thinking at least I had a very good excuse. In fact, I could claim that I almost killed myself because I was so dedicated to the project.

Mr. Warner was in a bad mood. He couldn't raise the money. The project was on hold—indefinitely. He'd send me some expense money and would be in touch.

I did get the money. He wasn't in touch. How fleeting fame.

The next year, for a reason long gone in my mind, I sold the car.

I was pleased because I had been making enough money to fund myself when next I would want a car and my uncle was pleased both because I had paid him back and he was sure he had taught me a life's lesson more important than anything I was learning in school. He hadn't, because if I had kept that $1,700, perfect condition, red, VW convertible, it would be worth today around fifty-grand. With economics, you have to learn all the lessons.

WILLIAM A. GRALNICK

*"Communism is cholera and you
cannot compromise with cholera"*

– Synman Rhee, first president
of the Republic of South Korea
and founder of GW's Korean
Institute, received his AB
degree in 1907, a distinguished
service award in 1947, and an
honorary doctorate in 1954

The Saddest Story

. . . One can go only so far running from someone in a train car.

Clowns have sad faces. The famous Greek masks are a pair, one happy one not. Except for what you might feel for me as I bumble from being the *schlemiel* to the *schlimazel* (the guy who spills the soup and the guy upon whom the soup is spilled), this book is presented to you as a happy romp through the college phase of my life. Not this story. It is a heartbreaker.

She was introduced to me by her roommate who was a friend of mine. Her name was Misty. She came from Nebraska. I would soon learn she was sweet, soft-spoken, affectionate, and fun to be with. She wasn't a Siren in looks but she was as pleasant to look at as she was to be with. I was also soon to find out she had serious problems.

We did a lot of walking and talking and going to classes together. We'd meet up at parties and later in the relationship (and mind you "later" in a college relationship, like summer camp, could be a matter of weeks) we were dating. It seemed like *Brigadoon* had descended around us. Foggy Bottom Washington could be every bit as romantic at night as Paris. That too helped.

Early on, Misty told me that she needed to be honest with me (never something one wants to hear . . .). First, she was rich. Her father had designed an article of clothing that was so popular it was swept off the racks faster than they could make them. Being suddenly rich wasn't as easy or as much fun as one might think, she intimated.

Next came the tragedy. She had a baby brother, toddler type, and a dog. She, the dutiful teenage daughter, took them out for a walk. The details were fuzzy but somehow a car careened around the corner wiping out child and dog. She stood there in shock, the dog's leash hanging from her shaking hand.

This had happened not too long ago from the telling of it. Her family wasn't comfortable with her leaving home to go to school but thought maybe it would be best to remove her from the horror show that had happened in front of her house. They contacted the health service and she wanted me to know she was in counseling. Like the mist she was named for, at times she would drift away, being there but not being there. At times, I felt if I reached out to touch her, my hand might go right through her.

As is often the case, piles of problems can make winsome worrisome, looks and overall personality not as prominent. The relationship that seemed perfect inexorably began to slip away. The coming and going of her blues began to take a toll on me as did her occasional night of binge drinking. I had a decision to make. Winter break I told her when we came back to school, we needed a time out. She was hysterical. That winter we had a siege of snow, the airports closed, and I had to take the train back to DC. The day before departure, Misty called sounding like her old self. "Hey. I guess you're taking the train too. Let's meet up. I'll find you. In mid-objection, she hung up. The next day, it was with trepidation that I boarded the express train back to school.

Sure, as promised, while curled in a seat and watching what passes for scenery as the train slipped out of Grand Central and rolled through upper Manhattan and the Bronx, there came a rap, rap rapping on my shoulders. Misty had found me. I knew I had to make this surgically sharp. I got up, put my hands on her shoulders, and said, "You shouldn't have done this. We both have things to work on. For a while, we're done." The reaction was akin to a mother seeing her child murdered. The scream of "Oh no! You can't do this!" was made ever more piercing, as it bounced off the narrow confines of the train car. Stunned, I took off down the car, through the connecting passage, and into the next car. She was in hot pursuit, decibel level rising. We had this *Maury Povich Show* argument going on except the stage was hurtling along at sixty mph and all the words went back and forth over my shoulder. And we did have an audience.

It should go without saying that one can go only so far running from someone in a train car. Eventually looms front or the back. At that point, you either jump or turn-around. The argument that had been going south to north now was headed north to south. By this time, we had picked up more fans. May my tongue cleave to the roof of my mouth and my right arm whither if people weren't yelling advice, hootin' and hollerin', some even clapping. Frankly, it was embarrassing. And exhausting. As we slid into Union Station, I grabbed my bag and like a Jack London character, mushed through the snow to my four-wheeled, yellow cab sled. Alone, I arrived at the dorm.

Don't go away. This isn't over.

That night, my friend, the one who introduced us, called me. Misty was caught trying to jump out the window. Several girls hauled her in, but she was out of her mind. Could I come over? Why me instead of 911? Maybe it was the right call. I got to the dorm, got upstairs (How that happened I don't remember), and I calmed her down. Of course, the calming took some compromise and while she was back on the room side of the window we were also back in a relationship.

For a few weeks, all was well. It seemed like I had had a nightmare set on a train. Now, I was awake and back in *Brigadoon*, until a random meeting on the street. I was leaving class and had to pass the medical center on the way to my next stop. There was the portly, smiling psychiatrist she was seeing and who I knew because he had done a few sessions of "couples counseling" with us. We stopped and chatted.

As if I was "on the couch" so to speak, I blurted out some questions. Did the death of the baby and dog leave such scars that they were unhealable? She had been nervous about an unexpected dinner with her parents who flew in, private jet, to see how things were going for themselves. How did that go? Of course, I didn't know I shouldn't be asking him these questions and of course he couldn't answer them. What he did say was, "Whoa!" What baby? What dog? What dinner? None of it was true. They were all stories designed to keep me where she wanted me. In an earnest, foreboding tone, he said to me, "Son. You're in over your head. You need to end this relationship—now! Come see me if you need help." My brains were scrambled like an egg.

Again—Don't go away. This isn't over.

Another conversation was to be had. The results were worse than the window scene. Misty went out, got drunk, and was gang raped. The next day, an ambulance plane took her home. She dropped out of school for the semester and entered a residential care facility. I was shaken to the core.

There's a finale coming.

That summer, the summer that followed my flunking the three major pre-med courses that occasioned the famous South Carolina Withdrawal Manifesto (see *War of the Itchy Balls . . .*), I went to summer school, changed my major, and rescued my GPA with five A's. One unusually tolerable summer day, I decided to take my books down to the Potomac River (there was a time when there was nothing but grass from the Lincoln Memorial/Memorial Bridge up to Georgetown's Key Bridge). Students flocked there to watch rowing teams practice, to sleep, make out, or in my case, study. It's all concrete and history now—Watergate and the Kennedy Center. As I breached the sidewalk and stepped on the grass, I noticed the back of a familiar body wearing a familiar outfit. It was Misty, prone to wearing Madras; it was clearly her. She had returned to make up her credits.

We talked softly, apologetically, and sadly.

We said goodbye and with a buss on the cheek, disappeared forever from each other's lives.

HOT PANTS:

A Short Story

. . . *the heat of the oven would dry them.*

Three frat guys getting ready for a prom isn't too much different than three girls doing it. Chaos reigns. Actually, then it was probably a bad idea when the three of us, known by our friends as *"The Three Musketeers"* because we were always together, decided to use the apartment one of us had moved into for the preparations.

It made sense on the surface. One of us had the car we were all going in with our dates. The apartment, unlike dorm rooms, had two showers not one. The rest was like organizing a troop movement. Who was supposed to be doing what and at what time: shower, shave, use the mirror, get dressed, have dinner (order in pizza). But even in professionally overseen troop movements a lot goes wrong and so it was with our highly unprofessionally overseen one.

What screwed up everything was that the one of us who had the apartment suddenly had a fit. He realized he had no clean underwear and he was of the type that wouldn't wear yesterday's. Hence right from the jump, we were off schedule. The second issue was the pizza. It arrived lukewarm. No big deal, throw it in the oven, heat it up, and eat. Pizza being pizza, if you were careful you could get a lot else done while downing it. So, quarters went into the washer then dryer, the oven was cranked up, and soon the apartment was bathed in the scents of eau de cologne and eau de pepperoni. Then came the next issue. Its significance was that the underpants weren't dry, and we were past the time that he should be wearing them.

Not everyone is a genius. None can be faulted for it. Thus, in retrospect, the genius of a solution he came up with wasn't lacking only in genius. It was lacking common sense. No time for the dryer cycle and if I recall correctly, we'd discovered a scarcity of quarters. But . . . the oven was warm. Lay the underpants and undershirt on the racks of the oven and the heat of the oven would dry them. Hey, some smarts. The fly in this ointment was he hadn't turned off the oven from heating the pizza nor did he clean the pizza laden racks. No one else thought of that either.

About twenty minutes later added to eau de cologne and eau de pizza was eau de burning cotton. By the time it hit one of our sets of nostrils setting off a Keystone Cops assault on the kitchen, it was too late. Both the underpants and the undershirts had scorch holes in them, and the undershirt was a poor imitation of prison garb having brown lines running across it. Then too there were bits and pieces of bubbled cheese, small spots of pepperoni oil, and a drop here and there of tomato sauce.

There's a reason this clothing is called underwear, it's under your other clothing so no one can see it.

Thus, with the placing of some additional eau de cologne here and there, problem solved.

He wore it.

We were late but off we went.

End of story.

GW Gym: "The Tin Tabernacle"

Our president thought that if it was good enough for the army to exercise in, it would make a perfect gym for the university—especially at no cost.

You're

IN THE

What Now?

"Hey! You! Agamemnon! Try your other right!"

"Why?" would be a good question to ask. "Why did I enlist in Air Force ROTC?" Yes, it was the only branch of service with an ROTC on campus but that's incidental information. I could also tell you that in high school, in our senior year, they added drill marching to the gym curriculum. I don't know the why of that either. Nor did I know that I was mildly dyslexic, which was the reason I marched like Bud Abbott (Abbott & Costello) in *Buck Privates*. I do know that at one point when I became like a salmon swimming against the stream with the other cadets coming at me instead of my going with them, the sergeant pointed in my direction and said, "Hey! You! Agamemnon! Try your other right!"

I think the reason we were out there was that GW didn't really have a gym. We had a real Army surplus quonset hut. The Quonset hut got hot as a roasting pan and I didn't want roast. Except in inclement weather, the cadets drilled outside. Not great but better than the hut. This joining ROTC fell into the category of "it seemed like a good idea at the time." It was a mistake albeit a short-lived one.

On the first day of class, we were to present ourselves at "headquarters." To say that "headquarters" was a dump would be overly polite. I had trouble finding it because it was actually an old (read "very"), old, two story house set back behind two more recently built large cement buildings. The officer's quarters were on the first floor, the quartermaster's lair was upstairs—literally. On the side of the house, a wooden staircase and door had been built. The exertion it took to get up the stairs should have tipped me off to something; it didn't. Trying to make "an entry," I ran the staircase which for reasons known only to the carpenter had dozens of steps equally separated but for the last. That one was more of a lip than a step, just high enough to catch your toe on, which I did. Suddenly, I felt I was in the Air Force. I had taken flight, flying right into and through the screen door; it did nothing to slow me down. I came to rest having made a perfect clip block on the master sergeant—you know, the sergeant with all the stripes on his sleeve that point up and all the others under them that point down? As he rested upon my prone body, he said, "Son, are you sure you want to go through with this?"

What followed reminds me of *The Phil Silvers Show* (Sergeant Bilko) of years gone by when a chimpanzee was inducted into the army. Here we go for a "how?" as opposed to a "why?" Call it a comedy of errors reaching the point of producing hysterical laughing during the foot exam. But at the beginning, the chimp follows the line of inductees behind a curtain for lower extremities examination. Someone calls out, "State your name!" There is no answer. Again, the command. Then someone says, "Hey, speak up!" The next in the chain of command yells, "For the record, Pvt. Harry, speak up!" It made sense to me because at Ellis Island my very hirsute great uncle played this scene. One guard takes a look at him and says, "What's that?" Another responds jokingly, "It's a bear." A third, paying no attention at all but to his task writes down on my uncle's entry papers, "Name: It'sabear Whatitwas." Truth.

The uniform process is very uniform. A line of us snakes through rows of shelves where there are upper classmen doling out pieces of uniform. You have no idea how many articles it takes to make a fully uniformed cadet. First question: "What size shoe do you wear?" With the response, you are handed a box with shoes in it. "Collar size and sleeve length?" The shirts are placed on top of the shoebox. Pant Length? Woven from wool that not only could keep out the cold, but could keep out anything, these unbelievably heavy pants are folded in half and placed on the shirts and in turn have laid over them the jacket that goes with pants. Close to the end comes the *piece de resistance*. It is an overcoat, the weight of an entire sheep. The upperclassman perused me, saw no natural resting place for it and said, "Stick out your fingers." On two of them he hung the hanger holding the overcoat.

Mind you, it is September. I won't go into the geography of the District of Columbia; I'll just say that it is one of the most humid cities in the country and the quartermaster didn't rate air conditioning. I began to feel a little woozy and began to wobble, my Leaning Tower of Pisa of clothes beginning to lean first one way and then, as I corrected my stance, the other.

I could see the door. One more stop to go. And what is the last thing we're given? All this little shit, each on a cardboard square that gets stuck in various places, on the uniform. They were the straw that broke the camel's back. I leaned, I tipped, I over-corrected; something began to slide off the pile. Reflexively, I grabbed for it. Picture everything I just described flying up in the air and then spreading out as each picked a somewhat different flight to separate floor landings. On hands and knees, I scrambled around scooping up things as fast as possible, until I came nose to toe with a pair of brilliantly shined shoes. They belonged to the same Master Sergeant who again cast doubt on my choice of course. Was it courtesy or a prayer that he offered me again the chance to hang it up and pick another elective?

At the beginning of this saga, I said my stay in the Air Force was short lived. It was. After a few classes in military stuff, came time to learn how to march. We used a part of the mall that was being re-sodded and at that point in time was, let's say, a dust bowl. Not only did Agamemnon reveal himself again but so did my asthma. The more dust I inhaled the less air I exhaled until one of my fellow cadets said something like, "I think this guy is gonna die. Tell the Sergeant."

It was with mutual relief that papers were signed decommissioning me. I flew off into the wild blue yonder, with the Sergeant waving joyfully as I departed.

"The greatest power a teacher has is the power of example. The way he runs his classes, lectures, grades, and deals with individuals should reflect his beliefs. He must practice what he preaches to his students as this makes for the good relationship between them."

– A. E. Claeyssens, professor of literature, produced 20 shows on public television, numerous awards

ROTC

Photo: Walter F. Krug, Washington, DC

PART THREE:

Higher Education

Introduction

"A professor is someone who talks while others sleep." *(WH Auden, 1940)*
But not all.

There were only a few ways one could get a bead on what college was supposed to be. One was school propaganda. Another was your parents' descriptions of their experiences tying their horses to posts on their campuses . . . or the stories of an older sibling. To this point in life, I always relied on my older brother. This time not. He had flunked out and ended up in night school. What I had were my fantasies.

My high school teachers told me high school was different from college. In high school there were expectations of the students. Not so in college. Didn't do your homework? Didn't prepare for a quiz? That's on you. Excuses? Mostly a waste of breath.

Yet I had this vision of the intellectual castle on the hill, even though parts of GW were below water level, the city having been built on a swamp. There would be austere purveyors of knowledge. There would be mind-enhancing challenges. One would learn to think.

Mostly, I was wrong. They call it fantasy for a reason.

The reality of college didn't hit me until classes started. When that happens, it begins to dawn on most students that:

- They'll be lucky if they can see the professor from their seat no less get to know him.

- That the professor knows that and doesn't much care.

- Taking notes is important and near impossible if, like me, you took what was essentially dictation.

- Noting that from the numbers of students who were asleep or hung over, the standard orientation speech pointing out that one or both of the students sitting next to you wouldn't be there next year was right.

One also learns from the grapevine and fraternity/sorority brothers and sisters that some professors are stunning lecturers and as stunning as some were many were a lot less so, coming close to deadly boring.

Here we will meet some of both. Professors who made indelible impressions on my life because some were so good, they were unforgettable, and some so bad they were equally unforgettable. A few fell in between. And at least two were definitionally "characters," sort of like from *Mad Magazine*.

We'll start at the beginning with my first lecture hall. It was biology and the professor was one of those characters. I'll make the introductions and then we will trip through political science, chemistry, physics, American History, American Literature, and one lab section that had more to do with the medical center than the subject.

"Hitch up your drawers" as this first professor would say, "set yourself in your seat," and let's go learn something in college.

There's interesting, and there's Dr. Munson.

And So It Begins

. . . I looked at my first professor and thought, "This is going to be very strange." I was right.

My first class was a lecture hall for Biology 101. I'd never been in a room with 300 people that wasn't a sports arena. Now I was and the score would have a lot more personal importance. Buzzing began to well up from the back of the auditorium. I turned, looked at my first professor and thought, "This is going to be very strange." I was right.

A short, squat fellow wearing somebody else's clothing, or so it seemed, walked in the door and ambled down the center aisle. I was to learn that entrances would be something to look forward to. Sometimes the dress of the day was a kilt, sans bagpipes. Sometimes it was a long shirt and longer shorts. The professor, a world recognized expert on things from foreign places that make most people go, "E-oooo!," had been known to tie a "leash" onto to the world's largest species of roach and fly it into class. The leash must have been a multi-purpose one because he also had leashed a slug the size of a soft-ball and wheeled it in an American flyer wagon giving it an entrance fit for royalty. I watched entranced as he, with some considerable effort, got himself up on stage and to the podium.

This first day, his introduction was such that it has stuck in my mind ever since. In a deep, and I do mean deep, southern drawl, he announced, "Mah naime is Sam C. Munson—p'fessa b'ology. An yowr stuck with me!" No hello. No nothing. Just that and the beginning of the lecture.

Dr. M. also taught the lab sections. He was good at it and close enough that you could make out what he was saying. However, a visit to his private laboratory was like stumbling onto an EPA contamination site. All over every possible space on which something could be pasted, taped, or otherwise affixed were signs in large letters warning the cleaning crew—"no sprays, no chemicals, don't even clean, I'll do it myself" signs. The fact was with one spray of bug spray, hundreds of thousands of dollars of grant money would disappear in a chorus of little voices shrieking, "RAAAAID!"

There were some other notable first day class openings.

Professor Peter Hill, American History: "I give one A a semester. Who do you think will get it?"

Professor Hugh Linus LeBlanc, Political Science: "This may be political science, but the language of currency in this class is English. Don't forget it."

My physics professor who I'm sure had a name but not one I remember other than it began with "Dr." and that's how he expected to be addressed. "My job is not to teach you physics. My job is to keep you out of med school."

It got much better with my French and Spanish professors. Different as two pieces on a chess board, they were both really interesting guys. Professor Metivier looked like a Professor Metivier should look, very continental, very French. His other job was teaching French at the Department of State to officials being posted to French speaking countries.

My Spanish Professor, Dr. Gio Mazzeo, looked, well, very Bronx. That's not a province of Spain but one of the boroughs of New York City. Prior to taking us on, he had been a senior translator at the United Nations and had done his doctoral thesis on the differences between coastal and inland Spanish. Put differently, he explored why some Hispanics spoke so fast they either didn't pronounce parts of their words or parts of the words never caught up with the rest of the sentence, while others spoke Spanish pretty much at the tempo with which Americans speak English. Really interesting stuff, but not relevant at the moment.

What is relevant is that both men loved their language and loved to teach it. They took away the fear that many Americans had of foreign language. "There is no better feeling than to be able to speak to a person in their own tongue." I've had multiple experiences to confirm that including patching together some Italian on a bus in Rome and having the bus driver embrace me with one arm and yell to anyone who could hear him, "Hey, thisa American kid, he speaka Italian!!" Everyone clapped. Or the bus driver in Martinique who was so enthralled by my awful French that he came to his next stop, threw everyone off his jitney, including bags and a few chickens, and took me home to meet his wife, who he would have make me lunch.

And they were kind men. First semester, I got an A in French but a B in Spanish. In the back of my exam book was a note. "Mr. Gralnick. You answered the last essay question in French. The French was perfect, but this is a Spanish exam, and I can't give you an A when you've used the wrong language." Hard to argue with that.

So, we were off and learning. It was weird getting used to not having homework, not having weekly or monthly quizzes. The semester was a straight line with two dots on it. One was midterms, the other finals. Those who thought they had a lot of time on their hands usually ended up doing poorly. Those used to cramming for tests in high school found themselves feeling like marathoners not quite sure if they'd make the finish line.

Those who managed to find a balance found they did about as well as they had in high school, usually a little worse but not much, and also found the wisdom that there was as much to be learned outside the classroom as in it. Those are the ones who had a well-rounded college life; I was fortunate to be one of them. Since most of us were seventeen, like me, or eighteen (but for Spencer) free time amounted to pledging a fraternity if you were so inclined and looking for dates. One usually joined a fraternity because as a freshman you learned that most girls on campus back then didn't want to be seen with you, so you needed a fraternity to break down that barrier or meet some brothers who had sisters in high school or sisters with friends in high school. For them dating a "college man" was a big deal.

Dr. Hugh Linus LeBlanc, The Louisiana Flash; great teacher.

Dr. Peter Hill, he gave me an A.

Notable Professors—

I Had A Few

He escaped his native "Loosiana" on a freight train.

Next, we come to poli sci and the school legend, Dr. Hugh Linus LeBlanc. He was a multi-legend—he escaped his native "Loosiana" on a freight train while the minions of Gov. Huey Long, with whom he'd had some political differences, were in hot pursuit. He played golf, for money, every available minute he had, and when he wasn't doing that, well . . . I'll stop there because he's still alive, well into his '90s and probably has a lawyer.

His entry into the first lecture wouldn't provide any mistaken identities with Dr. Munson. Starched shirt, tie, loafers, jacket and slacks—all the time. It was all delivered in pure southern drawl.

He was a brilliant lecturer. He was in constant motion. He accentuated important points with a clap of his hand, he spoke rapidly; it was almost all spell-binding. Nor was he shy about calling out a student who wasn't paying attention. No one dozed off on Dr. LeBlanc. I took every course he taught, and he was my master's degree thesis advisor. Before we leave him there are three interactions with him, I should share.

In my senior year, I decided I'd like to be a CIA agent. Mind you, coming from a background where it is said that a Jewish secret is anything fewer than 200 people know, it was probably an ill-advised idea. When I went to see Dr. LeBlanc for his opinion, he just rolled his eyes. I figured what the hell and went for orientation. The orientation ended with, "Now you may not tell anyone you were here—not your mother, your brother, or your roommate. If you do, we'll find out."

This was not going to work. They scared me half to death. I didn't go back for the test.

A more palatable thought was joining the Foreign Service. I spoke two languages. I had taken courses on Communism, Russian Government, South American Government. Why not? Again, I went to see my advisor. This time he talked. He said, "Bill you're a Jew from New York. If you don't mind spending your career being posted to the wilds of Africa or Outer Mongolia, it's a great idea." Point taken.

Next was my thesis subject. The Dixiecrat South was beginning to go Republican; I wanted to know the who, why, when, and where of it. Again, he spoke, longer this time. The message though was your subject will get you killed. The Deep South doesn't take kindly to northerners, especially Jewish college students riding in on a bus, using the "wrong" bathrooms, and asking a lot of questions. Hmmmmmm. Got it, Doc.

He had though a counteroffer. Just as the solid Democrat south was going Republican, the rock-ribbed New England states, led by Maine, were switching from Republican to Democrat. Leading the way was Senator Ed Muskie. I said, "How am I going to do research on this?" Again, the rolled eyes. "You're in the nation's capital. Each state has two Senators, and one of them in Maine is a Democrat. Go ask him."

Duh! So, I did, and it led to a lifelong memory, a set of experiences every political science student would kill to have. I called the Senator's office, explained to his secretary why I wanted an appointment, some of the details, and ended by indicating that without the appointment I might not get my degree. I got it.

On the appointed day, at the appointed hour, in the appointed place, I arrived. I was well-dressed and nervous as a cat at the National Dog Show. Finally, his secretary came out and basically said, "He's very busy and he forgot." I was crushed but God must love me because at that moment striding out of the office came this Lincoln-tall Senator of the United States. He asked what was going on and was terribly sorry when it was explained. But instead of giving me the ole W. C. Fields brush off, "Go 'way kid, ya bother me!" he said, Look, I'm very busy, but if you can keep up with me, I'll answer your questions during breaks and on the run. He said, "And awaaaaaaaaaay we go." No, he didn't, but that's what I was thinking.

I can't adequately describe what a hoot it is covering the ins and outs of the Senate of the United States and not have anyone challenge you once about anything. It's something, given Jan. 6, 2021, that will probably never happen again. He kept his word; I scribbled like a mad person. He even explained things on the Senate subway, his long legs hanging out of the car. It came to an end with these words. "Son, if you want the rest of the story you need to go to Maine and see Miss So and So who is the chief librarian in the state capitol. Everything you want to know will be in a box hidden away under her bed." Scout's honor, that what he said. For a semester, my life was lived in the Library of Congress and in my little, red VW driving to and from Maine on I-95. No computers, no GPS. Not even an IBM Selectric. I ended up with hundreds of index cards from which were born my thesis and never got lost for want of a GPS because I-95 is about straight as an arrow from Florida to Maine.

Every thesis director, no matter how nice, has a cruel streak. They are going to find something in your work that they want something more about. Dr. LeBlanc found one and the only way I could get the "more about" was to go back to Maine. This time, however, it was February. February in central and northern Maine is beyond cold.

I drove my little, red VW to Maine and rented a room in an old, drafty, boarding house. The room had no toilet, nothing I would call heat, a blanket and a sink. At 3 a.m., I awakened shivering and having need of the non-existent toilet. I wasn't about to go walking down the hall looking for the community toilet for my floor. Thank goodness for sinks.

Call me a liar but it was so cold that when I hit the streets for breakfast at 8 a.m., I found that my red VW had turned blue . . . I had breakfast, found my librarian, got my answer, and drove back to school. All of this to check one footnote.

Here's some more about the M&M boys, Dr.'s Metivier and Mazzeo. Dr. Metivier felt knowing French was only half the task, and the lesser half. Sounding French was what he wanted from us. He was so inspiring that I began to listen to speeches, endless though they were, by Charles de Gaulle who had the same attitude about French as Metivier. I walked around talking French to myself applying De Gaulle's accent to my pronunciation. Another A.

Mazzeo was another kind of bird. He dressed not like he taught Spanish but like he was from the Bronx, which, as I said, he was. His PhD was on the economics of Spanish pronunciation, what kind of commerce people did and how it affected how they spoke. In sum, if you worked on a dock, at a port, in a busy commercial district you spoke Spanish fast—like Cubans and Puerto Ricans, often lopping off the beginning and the ends of words. Inland people spoke more slowly and distinctly. That's what he wanted.

His gift wasn't making you pronounce things correctly, though he said if he ever heard anyone pronounce the name of the Garcia y Vega cigar as Garsha Vega, he'd flunk them no questions asked. His gift was making you love speaking a foreign language. His line, "There is no greater thrill than speaking to a man in his own tongue" has been a guidepost for me my whole life. He was so right. The appreciation from the listener is heart-warming and ego-boosting (except in Paris . . .).

I remember his talking about the wonders of Spanish. He said take the word cat, *gato*. In English, he said in English, to describe someone scampering across the roof like a cat you'd need all the words I just used. In Spanish you'd say he was *"gateando."* I was hooked.

Like LeBlanc, he was a wise man. All told I took five years of courses in four years from him. Came my senior year, I enrolled in his course on Don Quixote in Spanish. He called me up on the phone when he saw me as registered and asked, "Do you really want to torture yourself in your senior year with this course? Wouldn't you prefer taking advanced conversation, a course you can do something with rather than study a story written hundreds of years ago, in a foreign language, and is hundreds and hundreds of pages long? Message received, along with an A.

Mazzeo had another gift. He remembered things, maybe coming from the fact that he was for years a senior translator at the UN. About ten years after graduation, I read in the school bulletin that he received an award. I wrote him with the opening line, "You probably don't remember me . . ." He replied, "Remember you? You were the student who moved into an apartment that had a red door and was across from where they were building the Watergate complex." He was right. I was floored.

He also remembered that he had given me a B first semester and why. Ten years ago!

Maybe the most memorable of the group was my professor of religion. He was a Methodist minister. God forgive me. His name is gone. His opening line was unforgettable. "I'm probably not going to be here to give you your final exam. Pause. I'm dying of cancer." Talk about inspirational. Week by week we watched him diminish in size and strength. Week by week we were touched by his obvious love of God and his certain belief that religion, anyone called their own and were faithful to, made you a better person. True to his word, he was not there to give us the exam. He had died but he died loving teaching and loving the Lord.

I had other good professors. Let me introduce you to a few who were not. We'll start with the German Demon, Herr Wolfgang

Krause. Krause was a professor of philosophy at a university in Germany. Don't ask me why I was taking philosophy. I hated it. It made no sense to me, like Maritime law. I don't like things that don't have specific and enforceable answers. The schedule at GW and his home university didn't jibe. He was known then not to show up the first week of class and he had to be back the week that was our study week. That's when he gave us our final while we were studying for all the others. Not only was that hateful, but what he did to us was hateful. An old-style European professor, he'd have a student stand up in front of the lecture hall and he'd ask a question. If you were slow to answer, he ripped into you, often calling the respondent a dummkopf. If you answered incorrectly, you were verbally, publicly incinerated.

And there was his mode of dress. He wore sport coats of such heavy wool, I would break out in a sweat just looking at him. With this coat but bearing no attempt to match anything, was a tie, always the same tie, or he had a rack full of them. It was the '60s, the days of skinny ties. His was easily three to four inches across, scotch plaid, and again such heavy wool I wondered how his head, topped with a distractingly unkept mop of hair, managed to hold it up. I received a B. I was philosophical about it, but I never really understood how or why.

A professor whose name I don't remember and who was shockingly awful was my professor of Latin American Studies. His attitude was so colonial that I thought he'd come in one day wearing a conquistador's uniform. His attitude towards Latinos was they all should be picking bananas. And his second job? Teaching at the Department of State. In college, you learn, like Sam Rayburn told a young Lyndon Johnson, "in order to get along, you have at times to go along." I had to give back on exams this racist tripe he gave us during his lectures. Today, he wouldn't last a semester. The only A I got that I was embarrassed about.

That's the way it was. It seemed I either got A's or F's, fortunately a lot more of the former than the latter. I did get one D to go with the F's, but all my D and F professors were good professors. I just didn't understand what the hell they were saying. In both Physics and Qualitative Analysis, I got an A in lab. The math to explain what I did . . . fuhgeddaboudit. I learned more things in physics than any class I ever failed. The problem—surprise—was the math. I even got a tutor, one of the girls from one of the sororities who was a math whiz. I ended up with such a crush on her that sitting next to her, her arm occasionally brushing mine, I couldn't concentrate on what she was trying to teach me. I knew what was happening in the experiments but could not explain it in math. It wasn't until years later that I was told that I had mild dyslexia. Explained a lot.

Edwin L. Stevens, American Lit, a less likely looking comedian you're not likely to find.

Dr. Vincent: Taught me a ton. Flunked the course.

THE GOOD AND THE BAD—

Two More Professors

One could have learned a lot from the other.

Here are two more profs, one an old hand who really knew his craft, the other a newbie who thought impressing us was his job.

Let's start with the second one since I don't remember his name. He was young, a few years past his PhD, a social scientist who was surer than we that he was going places. He was bright, sharp, good-looking, and caustic. He taught political theory, which on a good day is well . . . so boring that it caused me to leave my own PhD program and take a job dealing with political practicality as Executive Aide to the Mayor of Stamford, Connecticut.

Only one thing I learned from him has stuck. Not a great percentage rating. The problem was I am about to explain it in this paragraph. It took him about six classes. It is called the zero-sum game. Poker is a zero-sum game. In politics, unless you've got what would be comparable to a Royal Flush, zero sum is to be avoided like the plague. It is replaced by negotiating.

What is a zero-sum game? Simply this: one person wins—everything, one person loses—everything. That's why if you are debating a nuclear disarmament treaty you want to end up as near to the middle as possible because if you lose—everything—

more than the game could be over. I don't know how many more examples it takes than those, but he felt it took a lot. And by the way, annoying or challenging him? That too was a zero-sum game.

Then there was Dean Elmer Louis Kaiser of blessed memory. At the time I was at GW, Kaiser had been teaching longer than I had been alive. He didn't stop until he was ninety, and not because he had dropped dead. I had heard that almost every course he taught was over-subscribed. I only took one, near the end of his career. It was held in the largest lecture hall on campus and not only were all the seats filled, students sat on the steps from the top of the hall down to the stage.

The dean was sort of gnomish, especially at that age in life. He was the kind of person who seemed to have been born smiling and never stopped. He was an animated lecturer with a resonant voice. He had a great sense of humor and felt a joke here and there in the lecture not only was fun but helped students remember the point he was making. It is a technique I myself have employed in my own lecturing. It works and by and large the students love it.

Because he didn't want to quit just then but he couldn't carry a full class load, he came up with the idea of a one credit course, given once a week. One credit seems hardly worth the effort but in the world of grades, and trying to get into grad school, it was like a piece on a finger puzzle that could be slid into many a needed spot. The course, whose name I don't remember, was about the politics of the day. Each lecture was about the ins and outs of what was going on around us, in some cases, just blocks away, in the nation's capital. It was amazingly fascinating and fun. So much so that I stole the idea from him and have taught for years a course called, "Ripped from the Headlines" (another theft . . .) with the same focus as his.

You can't give much higher a compliment to a professor than to say you loved his style, learned from his teaching, and stole some of his material. As they used to say on *Hee-Haw*, "Saaaaaa-lute!"

Queen of Broken Hearts

PART FOUR

Girls

Watching all the girls go by . . .

Introduction

None needed. I mean isn't this why most red-blooded American college males really go to college?

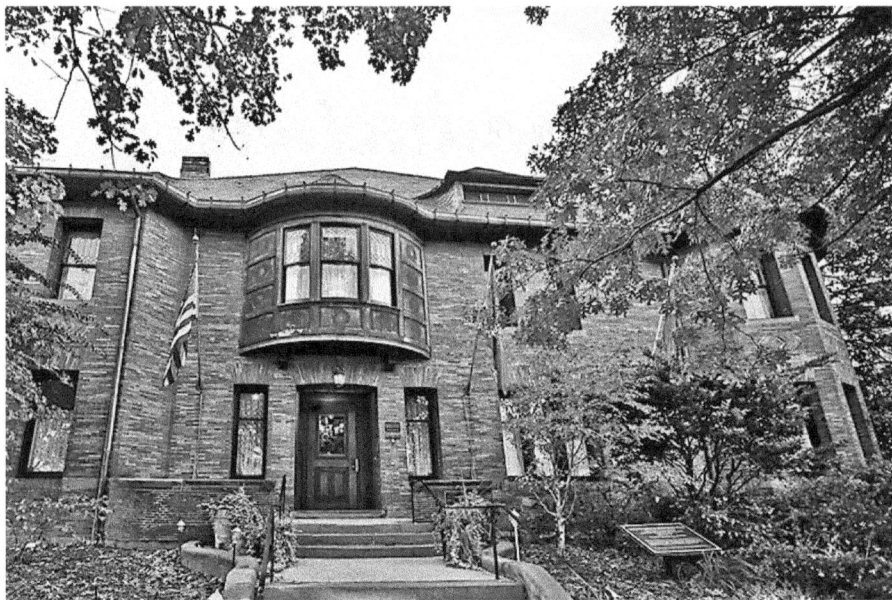

Michelle's house made this one seem like a cottage.

THE

Michelle

TOWERS

GW was quickly leaving behind its small, Southern oriented atmosphere. It was growing like mad. Gone was the "look for the cheapest paint" attitude. In was the real game of monopoly, as the university bought up everything its lawyers could get their pens on. Dorm space was at a premium and when right off the center of campus came available a small apartment building named "The Michelle Towers," it soon became the next women's dorm for the school.

One day at a fraternity party, I met a very cute girl whose name was Michelle. She was a high school senior. She was asking me about the university and when I told her of its newest acquisition, she blushed and said, "Michelle Towers?" "Oh, that's me." Her dad was a developer in DC and environs, and he named this opus after his only daughter. Hmmmmmm. That was interesting. And so was she. Flirty, friendly, and a lot of fun. I asked her out. Little did I know I was about to discover the American version of the class system.

For a high school senior, this filly was sharp and worldly. She was the kind of girl for whom boys lined up down the sidewalk in the hopes of catching her eye. But she wanted to be a high school senior who was dating a college man and that man, at seventeen years of age, weighing in at 135 lbs, was to be me. I was Jewish, so was she. We were both urban kids. For me it was cool. She had a high-end convertible and she'd pick me up at the dorm or the fraternity house. I got mucho points for that. We dated long enough that it was time for the parents to get curious, so she was given permission (or maybe was commanded) to invite me for dinner. She did. I accepted. How did I get there, being carless? I took a cab.

I took a cab that stopped in front of the largest house I had ever seen in my life. It was like a fieldstone fortress. My quick assumption was that the man of the house did very well building things and that Michelle Towers was sort of a Mickey Mouse project for him. It turned out the idea of naming something for his little girl came before he had something on which to put the name. With the name in hand, he built the apartment building. Oh, how daddies love their daughters.

The doorbell was found. It was shrouded in vines. I pushed it. It was one of those Big Ben sounds that began at the front door and pealed its way throughout the manse. Expecting Michelle to open the door, I was taken aback when this fellow in livery stood in her place. He half-bowed and welcomed me by name. That I thought was spooky since we'd never met. I stepped across the threshold and suddenly felt I was falling into the basement, that's how thick the carpeting was. It was so thick it was hard to keep your balance on it. Jeeves, or whomever, took my coat and led me into whatever it's called, the waiting room, receiving room, delivery room, the room you were put until someone came to take you to another room. I was offered a drink (soft) and told I would be fetched momentarily. If I needed anything before that I needed only to ask. Where he was going to be to hear me, I didn't know, but I decided just to let it play out.

Shortly, in bounced Michelle looking cute as a button. She took me into another room where we waited for Daddy Developer and his wife of the diamond ring like I couldn't believe. Were it not for the diamonds around her neck, I don't think my gaze ever would have gotten above her hand. Again, came the offer of a libation, this time the list of offerings included beer. I grabbed it. After a dutiful bout of chit-chat and information gathering (about me), a woman with a bell appeared. After the first tinkle, mother moved us towards the dining room to the longest table I'd ever seen. I was put at one end, father at the other, the women across from each other. I wondered if we got megaphones to enable conversation or if by the chair might be a closed-circuit telephone system so you could call whoever it was at the table you wanted to chat with. I was not comfortable and when one isn't comfortable one tends to make blunders. Let us say I was a blunderbuss of errors, large and small, during this inquisition of a dinner.

There was once in my life a woman who worked for my family named Mrs. Curtis. Her goal in life was to teach me manners. That included when faced with a place setting fit for the queen, I would know what to use each utensil for. I could tell a fish knife from a regular one. What the stuff lined up above the plate instead of at the sides of it were for. Where one's glass was, and which side the butter plate was on. I needed all that knowledge. Honest to Pete, the place-setting was terrifying. The acoustics were good so I could converse fairly well with mother and Michelle. The botanical garden in the middle of the table made it hard to see no less talk to Dad. Probably good.

I don't tell a lot of people this, but I have a nervous bladder to go with what was then a nervous stomach. Came a time in between one course or another, I had to ask someone where the bathroom was. I just didn't know who to ask so I sort of signed to Michelle, she called Jarvis, and he led the way. He also waited by the door to lead me back. On the way back he politely whispered, "Young man, you might want to zip up your fly." Egad. I was in the open field so to speak. Why he couldn't have told me while I was still in the hallway . . . so I sort of leaped into my seat and waited for the cover of activity from the kitchen, servers with dishes that had silver covers, to surreptitiously drop my hands into my lap and pull up my fly.

I exhaled and we flew through the rest of dinner. Then disaster struck. Anxious to leave the dining room with Michelle, I jumped up and scooted over to her side of the table. Unfortunately, I was now attached to my side of the table. My place setting began to follow me like a golden retriever puppy. I had zipped the edge of the tablecloth into my zipper. As Lilly Tomlin's Ruth Ann used to say, "And that's the troot!"

Could it get worse? Yes.

It was the '60s. Those of my age looked down upon the upper classes of the world, butlers and all that jazz. We were all equal, man. Right? Wrong. So, when Pervis handed me my coat and said, "May I show you out?" I snubbed my nose at him and said, "No Thanks. I'll get the door myself. Thanks."

Regrettably, I then noticed that there was a virtual hallway of doors, each made of the same wood. I was trapped on the set of "Let's Make a Deal." Behind what door would I find the outside world? Door number one? Door number 2? Door number 3? I grabbed a handle, pulled open the door, and walked...into a closet. The answer was door number two. But you know, good ole Heathcliff, he didn't blink an eye. He politely said, "I believe you were looking for this one, sir." Upon his opening "this one" I saw the world. I was never so happy to hear the words, "Come. I'll drive you back to school," as Michelle came to my rescue.

How does one end such a saga? One says, "See Ruth Ann."

The Reputation

There are reputations and then there are reputations.

Back then if a girl "put out" or "did it," she didn't necessarily have a bad reputation, just a reputation. If she were a sloppy drunk and could make a bar stool blush, she had a different kind of reputation. Then there was Suzanne's reputation.

When a dozen guys would walk out of a lecture hall because someone whispered something in their ears and that something was where Suzanne and the bottle of bourbon were, when someone has the urban legend attached to her that she gave herself to the moving men because she didn't have money for a tip and never denied it, well that was a whole different kind of reputation and that reputation was Suzanne's.

It was a reputation that caused the Dean of Men to call a meeting of the fraternity council where he uttered the immortalized warning against invitations to Suzanne. He said, "Gentlemen, a stiff prick knows no conscience."

Kids like me we were afraid of the Suzanne's of the world, though near as I knew at GW there was only one reputation like that. Yet sometimes, you decide that you've got to man-up and give it the ole college try. One night, that idiotic thought came over me. I knew that when she wasn't with someone somewhere else, she was at the college's campus beer cabaret, the Rathskeller.

The Rathskeller was pretty much what you'd imagine a college campus bar was. It was pretty ordinary with a pass at trying to look like an off-campus bar. It was pretty much everyone's second choice. If you were in a fraternity, whatever it was doing was the first choice. If you weren't in a fraternity or sorority, anyplace off campus was your first choice. For people who had nothing to do and/or didn't feel like walking very far or finding a way to get to Georgetown, the "R" was it. I think Suzanne went there on nights she wanted to be left alone, do a little drinking, do a little flirting, sort of take a night off so to speak. It was on such a night I chose to try and get lucky.

I wasn't just going to wander in. I had just bought the most scrumptious feeling, black velour, zip-up from the mid-chest, long-sleeved shirt. I couldn't imagine anyone not wanting to snuggle up against that shirt. New jeans and shoe boots topped off the "Mr. Irresistible" outfit. In I strolled. The interesting thing about this girl/woman was that she wasn't pretty at all. Not ugly mind you, but no one the average guy would take a second look at. She was well-proportioned but didn't dress to show it off. And yet as I scanned the room and spied her, she was surrounded by guys filling her dance card—but nothing more.

It took about a half hour before there was a break in the action. I saw my chance and took it. At that moment, the band switched to slow songs. *God loves me*, I thought. We "clutched and hugged" for a song or two. She was smoking and I was trying not to choke. She bent backwards at the hip; it had an interesting effect on me. She looked me in the face, said, "What did you say your name was?" "Bill, I stammered. "Bill," she said, ". . . you can't handle me." It was very matter of fact. I mustered up my strength, steadied my voice and replied, "Don't be so sure." With that she came closer, giving off this electric magnetism. As I drew closer . . . she blew smoke in my face. Then she said, "Nice shirt," took her cigarette, and burned a small, round hole into it and my chest.

I said goodnight and left.

Beaten.

A
Hood Ornament
LIKE NO OTHER

*Some people used car hoods for suntanning—
she had other uses for them.*

Nothing good ever happened to me on our occasional scouting trips to the American University campus, just things that made wonderful stories to tell. Here's one.

Entry to the campus was preceded by a fairly ordinary parking lot and kids coming and going from class. As we slowly moved down the line of parked cars looking for one that was vacant, I was the first to see her. "Will you look at that!"

There, atop the hood of a red car, was a girl dressed in black leggings and a very tight blouse. In between her . . . er protrusions was a large, silver, Eastern Orthodox cross. I had learned that the year before in comparative religions. Her hair was black as night and shoulder length. Her lipstick was beyond red, neatly but thickly applied to lips that had that, "I'm really something to kiss" appearance. I don't know if someone can have black eyes, but hers seemed to be. She was stretched out full-length on the car with her upper torso using the windshield as a support. Yes,

Popular Mechanics and other magazines had lots of car ads always showing luscious models along with them. This "ad" did not speak of luscious. Lascivious seemed the better description. I remember all that and more about her, yet her name is gone.

Finally, there was a space, we piled out, agreeing to meet at a certain time, and scattered in different directions. Mine was arrow-straight right back to that car. Now a sophomore, I had a bit more confidence. I ambled up to the car and said, "Isn't that hot?" Her retort was, "No, but I am, all the time." That did it for my confidence. Let us call her Magda and begin the story.

We had a long talk that afternoon and several others as well. She liked to call me on the dorm pay phone in the hall, often after a date. I've never participated in phone sex but had I, those conversations seemed like they would be them. And it was so natural. In between the "how was your day?" and "any exams coming up?" were anatomical descriptions of her dates and how they measured up to her needs and wants. In short order, after someone yelled, "Bill, Magda on the phone," I drew a crowd of guys hopeful she would talk loud enough that they could hear her voice travel into my ear, through my head, out the other ear and into theirs. I was having my fifteen minutes of fame.

This is what I learned about Magda. She was from Monticello, NY. To the meat of it, one needs to know a bit about Monticello. First, it's small. The last census showed about 6,700 people. It's old, probably been there for centuries. Wikipedia listed eight famous people from Monticello. I've heard of none of them. It is famous for two things. The racetrack and its proximity to the part of the Catskill Mountains known as the Borscht Belt. Thus, it did a good business on Route 17, with travelers going to or coming home from summer vacation, as well as truck drivers, mostly loggers going from the forests to the mills. And it was home to Magda.

Magda was Hungarian. She was hot-blooded by self-description, explaining that all Hungarian women are. Her black hair was real as she showed me one day because she believed all the facts so to speak should be on the table. It was clear she had gorgeous legs, since her leggings seemed to have replaced her epidermis, they were so tight. As for the rest of it, this is how the truth came to be affirmed. We were sitting on campus and she was commenting on what girls did to make themselves look bustier. She pointed out who had "falsies" and who stuffed their bras. She said, "You gotta go with what you got." "This is what I got" and as part of the conversation she lifted her sweater up over her head to display a washboard stomach and a *Playboy* worthy upper body. It was done so nonchalantly I was non-plused. What does one say after seeing exhibit A? As I recall, I managed to squeeze from my vocal cords, "Yup. That's all you."

One day, she said to me, "Hey, your frat is having a party Saturday night. Why don't you invite me?" How she knew before I knew I didn't want to know. That she invited me instead of my having to endure the anxiety attack of having to ask her was a blessing. It was an odd night. We walked in and honest to Pete all the activity in the living room just stopped. Another fifteen minutes added to my ledger. And she was something to behold. Men often have favorite parts of a women's body that raise their interest. Some men call themselves ass-men (others speaking about them use another word instead of men . . .); other guys go for the legs. With the fame and fortune of Dolly Parton, you can guess what another category is. Some, looking at luxurious, long hair had dreams of how it would feel brushing against their face—or elsewhere. And for everyone, lips to kiss that were fulsome, thick with lipstick, and perfume that was mind-altering. Magda had it all and they all thought I had her. I didn't.

We were friends but the benefits were limited. For instance, that night I got some great dances and a very stimulating kiss goodnight. Enough for more phone calls and another date. Here we move from a party-setting to the back seat of a fraternity brother's car. We were going somewhere; I have no clue where. It was a long drive. My fraternity brother was with his main squeeze, someone I was about find out believed in Magda's mantra, you gotta go with what you got. She was very sweet, not too pretty, petite with about that much of a figure.

Magda, who was holding my hand in hers on my lap, was fixed on the rear-view mirror. Suddenly she leaned over close enough to my ear to get lipstick on it and said, "I knew it. I just knew it." "Look!" As I tried surreptitiously to sit up, I noticed I could not see the head of the girl in the front seat. Peculiar noises pervaded the car. In case I couldn't figure it out myself, Magda gave me a clinical description. "I'll be damned. She's giving him a blow job!" And she was. Magda said, "let's try that." Before I had a heart attack our driver announced we'd be at our destination in a few minutes. Subtract some fame minutes from the ledger.

Before we leave Magda, who dropped out of school, let me share one more tidbit. It's about the economic development of her hometown. The big reveal came in a conversation about our goals for the future. Far as I know, neither of us reached them. For me, decades later I know proof positive I didn't make mine. If you read, "War of the Itchy Balls . . ." you read about the train ride to hell where I typed a letter to my parents telling them I had flunked three science courses and was switching my major. They wanted me to be a doctor. I wanted to be a vet. Neither happened.

For her it was definitely a horse of another color. She wanted to open the first brothel in Monticello—I kid you not. She had thought it out pretty well. All those reasons why as a town Monticello became an economic hub, or hubette, I mentioned up the page a ways would provide ample revenue for her entertainment enterprise. She told me she was dropping out. She had gone to college to take some business courses and to, shall we say, practice the physical side of her craft. She had learned what she needed to on both accounts.

Who knows how it turned out? Up to that time I had never been to Monticello nor have I up to this time. So, if someone knows, it certainly isn't me.

"Senator, I am one of them. You do not seem to understand who I am. I am a black woman, the daughter of a dining-car worker . . . If my life has any meaning at all, it is that those who start out as outcasts can wind up as being part of the system."

– Patricia Roberts Harris, graduated #1 in class 1990, first African American Ambassador, first African American Cabinet Officer, member of Biden Administration, member of African American Women's Hall of Fame

I'd walk a mile with a camel.

I'D WALK A MILE FOR
A CAMEL—

Amy's Story

*She was one of those girls one had to take a
number and stand in line to talk to.*

To you it might seem like we've said plenty about girls, but there were plenty of girls. After all, isn't that why every red-blooded boy really goes to college?

She was a Jewish Lorelai. But again, I get ahead of myself. As soon as one drove onto the campus of American University, a few miles uptown from GW, one knew it wasn't GW. The student population was very "New York" and the girls were very "Long Island." That means they generally were sharper looking and pretty in a way that said, "Long Island" to a lip-licking kid from Brooklyn. For instance, you'd never drive through GW and see a dark-haired, long-legged dream wearing pants that looked like they could do damage to her circulation using the hood of a car as a bed and its window shield as a pillow. She was a real traffic stopper. And she knew it. But that was not Amy.

Amy combined the wholesomeness of someone you dreamed nice dreams about and the muted sex appeal that occasionally made the dream not-so-nice, or shall we say salacious. She was personality plus, smart, could have a conversation about anything, and was prone to shifting topics and gears on the fly so that the male or males she was bewitching at that moment were thrown off balance. Consequently, she was one of those girls one had to take a number and stand in line to talk to—not really, it only seemed so.

I don't remember how it came about, but one day my number came up. I had hung around, waited like in a deli, for my number to come up, and was impressing enough when I got the shot that she accepted a date with me. It was sort of a "walk in the park and have ice cream" kind of date. It was simple enough but for the fact that she was walking on the street and I was walking about eight inches above it. I took another shot, she said yes, and I decided to go the full Monty—fancy dinner and tickets to then the hottest movie showing, *Lawrence of Arabia*. By now, dear reader you should see how the camel mentioned above fits in.

It was a very long day and a very long movie. Unlike any other movie I had seen, it had an intermission. That was fine for me. It meant more time with her. We were cozy in the theatre. She let me put my arm around her. Occasionally, she would lean her head on my shoulder, her smells from perfume and hair stuff were intoxicating. There was no hanky-panky. My hand rested on her shoulder blade and a wayward finger was instructed quickly to stay attached to its hand and the hand stay attached to her shoulder.

Permit me a digression. I'm sure others have done such things, but every-so-often something came over me in the presence of intoxicating girls and I would do something that the average person could only call stupid. Freud would have seen it differently. Like the time I tackled my date on Coney Island Beach as she got up to run into the ocean. I tore the ligaments in her knee. Or the time I invited this real knock-out up to see my electric train set on the third floor of our house—and thought her acceptance meant that she wanted to see them. So that's what we did. Then she saw something light up on my body that flashed, "Hopeless" and said she had to go home. I've got a million of 'em, as Uncle Miltie used to say. I'd add, "unfortunately." And so it was with Amy.

In *Lawrence of Arabia*, the camel is a prominent player as one would expect on the sands of the Arabian desert. Somehow, the sound a camel makes got into my head. It is a sound that could be nothing but a camel. A guttural braying that has a donkey-like quality to it but much deeper. I doubt you find that of much interest, and I dare say that of the several hundred people in the theatre, including Amy, I was the only one who thought about it.

You know by now that there was a time in my life that I did some pretty mean imitations of animals. My blue-ribbon winner was the barking of a seal that went with my aforementioned interpretation of Snoopy being a vulture. Dog. Seal. I know it makes no sense. But in the theatre rather than concentrating on whether or not I could pull off some subterfuge that would get my finger past her shoulder blade, I was concentrating in my head on perfecting the bray of Lawrence's camel.

It gets worse because I did. And the ending is awful. Keep going.

We walked into the lobby during intermission and the spirit of Lawrence's camel overtook me. With no real thought (obviously), more of an impulse, I brayed. Loudly. Dozens of pairs of eyes turned towards me. One pair turned away.

I never saw Amy again. Well, that's not true. I had heard that she was living with a guy in a trailer at the edge of campus. He was older, gentile, and bore a striking resemblance to John Henry, the steel-drivin' man. One day, when I was back on the AU campus, I saw them. The notes of "There Goes My Heart" went through my head. I was about to call out to her, but this time I did think. I walked on.

Sometimes you just get it wrong.

CAN'T
Win
FER
Losin'

He produced her phone number and said,
"Go have a good time on me."

Unfortunately, I could write a dozen stories similar to this one. I won't, but I could. It's all part of what you don't learn in class. Sometimes you see the lessons coming and can decide how much if any you want to learn from them. Sometimes, you are blind-sided. Sometimes they are just strange, start to finish. This is one of those.

There was a guy we were friends with though he was not a fraternity brother. He was a nice guy, a little dorky, certainly no movie star in the looks department but he seemed to do exceedingly well with the girls. He did have a car. The first part of the lesson is obvious. There's no quantifying what a car on campus will do for someone. It did a lot. But this story isn't about him. It's about a tip from him.

I was between girl friends at school and had no one waiting for me in that department at home. Before winter break, we were BS'ing and he told me about this girl in his neighborhood who was good looking but a pariah. Here's the run up and where I'm gonna blow (no pun intended) the PG rating. This sweet girl had the reputation, as a friend of mine who was a vice cop used to say, "of being able to suck the chrome off a tailpipe." Sorry, but that's an exact quote.

So, when Richie heard my predicament, he produced her phone number and said, "Go have a good time on me." Now mind you this was 1962 or '3. The world, even a lot of college students in it, have matured since then, but not me. I got home and after enough days of family pleasantries, the weekend was upon us and I decided to make the call. My hand holding the number was sweating so much that I was afraid the number would be saturated, obliterated from sweat, and I'd lose it before I finished dialing. But I didn't and the call connected. Yes, I had the right number. Yes, she and Richie were friends though she hadn't seen him in a while, and no she wasn't busy Saturday night so sure she'd be happy to go to a movie.

There aren't many ways to explain the geography predicament unless you've experienced it. If you're from Chicago think Dan Ryan Expressway at rush hour. If you're from Los Angeles—the 405. In New York, we natives would get a laugh from real estate ads shouting that this or that new development on Long Island was only twenty-five minutes from the city. Why did we get a laugh? Because unless you were driving at 3 a.m. it could seem more like twenty-five hours. The traffic on the L.I.E. (Long Island Expressway) was bumper to bumper from the Mid-Town Tunnel to anyplace. And it would often take twenty-five minutes or more just to get into the tunnel. This girl lived on the Island. But the potential reward seemed well worth the traffic.

I didn't quite know what to expect when I rang the bell, but I let out a sigh of relief when she answered it. Certainly, a strong B if not a B+. She was a little nervous, personable enough, conversational enough. Off we went. Saw a movie, had an after-movie bite to eat then headed back to her house. I cannot honestly say I was concentrating on the driving, but we got there.

As we pulled to a stop, she turned to me. "I have something I have to tell you."

"Go right ahead," I said in my most soothing of voices. "I'm sure Richie told you all about me." I was silent as a submarine running the depths. "Well, I'm sorry, I don't do that anymore." I saw Snoopy the Beagle in an airplane flying by waving his fists and yelling, "Curse you, Red Baron!" She continued, "I hope you understand, and I want to thank you for a lovely evening. She leaned over, kissed me, opened the door, and was gone into the dark of her driveway. I had the Long Island Expressway, Brooklyn-Queens Expressway, and local streets to think this through.

I got home about 2:30 in the morning having decided that I had just had one of the saddest encounters of my dating life and the sadness wasn't mine. Hard to explain. I sensed I had just met a nice, young woman who couldn't run in the social race that was the chic, so-called five town area of Long Island. She either thought of or was told of a sure-fire way to fill up her dance card—probably by Richie . . .

Sad and true to form, instead of the promised "good time" I had sadness and guilt.

Maybe that says something for me—and about me.

Swimming
LESSONS

The house looked like a scene from, **My Big Fat Greek Wedding.**

During summer school, I seemed to have a lot of time on my hands. Because I had classes every day, I didn't have to study much. I had good retention. A friend belonged to a swim club and invited me for the day. Why not? While keeping my mouth shut, I was thinking upon arrival, "exactly as advertised—a swim club." It was not a country club with a swimming pool. It was a lot of cement and chairs with a swimming pool. It turned out, however, that it was a swim club with a goddess as a lifeguard. Please God. Let me drown.

No such luck but I did work up the courage to chat. Eventually, she had a break and climbed down from her perch and we continued the chat face to face. The view was no less enchanting than looking up at her. She was a high school senior from a wealthy family, was tall and fit because she was training for next summer's Olympics and altogether was so charming that the cross on her chest didn't seem quite as big as it did at first. Suddenly, I was a lot more interested in being invited back. She must have read my mind because as we parted, she said I could come anytime as her guest. All I had to do was tell the guard at the gate. Simple.

After several weeks of chatting and leering, I got an invitation to dinner. Now I don't know what this girl told her family about me but let's just say the house looked like a scene from, *My Big Fat Greek Wedding*. There were little children, and grandma the matriarch, brothers and sisters aplenty, a few friends, maybe the neighbors, and a few drop-ins known and unknown, and of course mom and dad. I don't do well in crowds of strangers and this was overwhelming. We did a doggy paddle around the room to get me acquainted and it was finally time to eat. It was Sunday so dinner was at three o'clock. Don't ask me. I'm Jewish. Apparently, that was the deal "chez them" on Sunday after church.

The doors parted like the Red Sea opening up on a dining room table, or probably two or three strung together that could have held both Pharaoh's Army and Moses' team. Aside from the noise, all I remember is green beans with canned onions and gracing the middle of the table a large, glazed pig, apple stuffed in his mouth. He had a mournful look in his eyes, eyes that were looking right at me. So how do you tell your hosts, who obviously had gone to a great deal of trouble and expense for their daughter and her date, that you don't eat pork, or a lot of other stuff on the table? Probably why I remember the green beans.

And the heat. All those people and all that hot food made the temperature in the room slowly begin to climb. I felt I was in a volcano whose lava was bubbling and boiling as it rose to the point of explosion. I realized then that the bubbling and boiling was my stomach, which had begun to do somersaults. I looked at the pig. He looked back with a, "Don't look at me, Buddy. This wasn't my idea" look. I was seated midway at the table. That way everyone could have a clear shot at me.

What they saw was this: as the red in the thermometer got redder, my face got whiter. As the temperature in the room rose, so did the contents of my stomach. A volcanic eruption was coming. Father, assuming a bodily need, kindly pointed me to the bathroom, but to get to it, I had to push by nineteen or twenty dozen people saying each time, "Excuse me please" and helping them scoot their chairs closer to the table. This was gonna be close.

With the grace of a figure skater, I opened the door, closed the door, and flipped up the toilet seat, seemingly all in one motion. Certainly a 9.7 score. Then I turned on the water as loud as it would run and wretched my guts up, until sweat was not only rolling down my face but seemed to be coming from spouts that had somehow been placed under my armpits. Weak as a pup, I was in worse shape than my friend on the table. He at least was dead; I knew I was going to live, would have to open the door, and return to mayhem. I inspected my mouth, shirt and pants for stray pieces of gunk and made my entrance to hundreds of eyeballs trying not to look right at me. My Olympic goddess whispered, "Are you all right?"

Maybe it was my mother. Maybe it was the cross. This was not meant to be. We never saw each other again. I heard through my friend that she too was punished. She didn't make the team. I was sorry. Guilt is a wonderful thing. I was sure it was my fault. And you know, somehow, it probably was.

"Nothing can stop the attack of aircraft except other aircraft.

         – Gen. Billy Mitchell, father of
         the modern Air Force, first
         man to land bombers on air-
         craft carrier, graduated in 1919
         and was also honored by the
         university later in life

A

Ghostly

NIGHT

It hit me finally that I didn't know where the hell I was.

Some dates, and parties, were so not worth the time that all I would remember about them had nothing to do with the girl. This one had to do with a ghost I either met or didn't meet after a date who lived in the middle of nowhere.

Mind you, I don't believe in ghosts. The District of Columbia has several buildings that supposedly have resident ghosts. I was a licensed tourist guide in DC. I never saw one. My disbelief was enhanced. It was sorely tested one college night.

Someone had lent me a car to go to a party. I was on the way home, but the way I was going less and less seemed like it would take me where I wanted. It hit me finally that I didn't know where the hell I was other than in the Commonwealth of Virginia and her northern suburbs. Then I began to doubt the suburbs part. I was on a road—alone. My headlights seemed to light up the car lanes to forever, but in that forever, there was nothing. No houses, no cars.

But there were bugs, lots of them flying around. Clouds of 'em. They didn't help matters as I thought, *what if I have to get out of the car?* And as a reminder—no such thing as a cell phone.

Why I do this I don't know but when I'm headed in a direction, even if it's the wrong one, I keep going. Maybe I think if I stay the course long enough, it'll become the right one. Maybe, as in this case, I was too freakin' freaked out to get out of the car. And what would I do if I did? It would have been me and the bugs on the road, so I kept going. More oddly, I hit the gas pedal so I could get to nowhere faster. Then came the moment where rationality and irrationality bumped into each other.

Way, way out in the reaches of my high beams was something. A deer maybe? I began to slow down and as I slowed weird took over. The slower I got the more like a person whatever it was that shone in my headlights appeared to be. My lights sharpened on the subject. Now I could see it was waving its arms—frantically. It looked like a person looks on a lonely country road whose car broke down and hasn't seen another in too long. But I didn't see a car, broken or "un." Maybe it (I hadn't yet been able to determine male or female) was in trouble—hurt, sick, or being pursued by someone it didn't want to be pursued by.

You've by now noticed I have begun to refer to this phantasmagoria as "it." I had slowed quite a bit and continued. The nearer I got, the less clear whatever it was was. No part of it said distinctively, "I am a man" or "I am a woman." It did have shape: tall and thin. It did not look like a sheet or a form with that long, oval mouth one sees today in cartoons that says ghost. Nor did its sleeves hang down in big bags—bags big enough to have held small animals. "Clammy" didn't cover the sweat that bathed me. What to do? What to do?

For a moment—brief though it was—I thought about stopping. I didn't. "Why?" Many reasons but mostly because of this one. At about twenty-five feet distance I noticed that my headlights were not creating a shadow as they washed across this whatever it was.

Worse yet, I thought I could see the beams behind the figure meaning—survey says—they were penetrating whatever it was. I began to increase my speed. It began to run from one side of the two-lane road to the other still frantically waving its arms. *Hell, I thought, if the beams are going through, I guess the car will too.* I was pretty certain—one is never surely certain when one is alone on a dark two-lane road—I would drive right through whatever it was. And yet, as I braced for the moment of possible impact, it leapt to the right, ran down an embankment, and disappeared into the dark. There was no sound. No bump or bang. There was no splash of blood. I sped up—quite a bit.

Mind you, I was sober as a judge. There are very few roads to no-where so it wasn't too much longer before I came to an intersection. It had all the requisite signs to give me my bearings and in about a half an hour, I was home. I did look over my shoulder once or twice as I walked into my apartment. I never came up with an explanation.

Maybe you can.

Meanwhile, never again would you find me driving alone on dark, country roads that seem to have no end even if there were a girl somewhere in the story.

"The only correct actions are those that demand no explanation and no apology."

– Red Auerbach, GW player and coach, world renowned coach, Boston Celtics student, player and coach M Ed 1939 and Honorary Doctorate 1993

THE *Girl*
WHO WOULD
BE A
Woman

"Wise beyond his/her years."

"Wise beyond his/her years." You've all heard that expression. You all know that boys and girls mature at different rates, girls being the faster of the two. Yet even with that fact, some girls become women even faster. This sets them apart. There were two in my life and they were connected.

My first sister-in-law was just wonderful even though she could be goofy in a fun sort of way. She was a reservation agent for an airline, during the days when booking or changing flights was done with the aid of gigantic books. No computers. I think that dealing with impatient people in a process that defied patience probably both grew her up quickly and taught her the value of well-placed humor. She was so wise and intuitive that it was almost forty years later that I realized she was only two years older than I. When I went off to college, she thought I could use someone not at GW, someone well educated, fun, with a gene for helpfulness. She introduced me to Lesley. I fell head over heels.

Lesley was also only two years older than I, but we were planets apart in maturity. I was a kid still growing up, she was a woman who in spite of her lack of years had already grown up. A great conversationalist, she was also a great listener. When she had advice, she offered it before she gave it. She had a great sense of humor and a lovely laugh. She dressed beautifully in a pert sort of way. She was very pretty but with a business-like look, except at night when she dressed her age. It didn't help (me) that her honey brown hair swept down over her forehead and across one eye. She was Archie's Veronica come alive. Of course, she was happy to be my big sister and introduce me to her roommate who for reasons I couldn't fathom had an instant, drop-dead crush on me. This is worth a digression.

When it became apparent that it was going to take some doing to get Lesley to realize that the wrong girl had been chosen for me, I decided to ask out the roommate, Janet. The first time I went to pick her up, I realized these were two very different girls having only personality in common. Janet was shall we say a bit top-heavy. She dressed like she didn't want you to miss that fact, which was perfectly fine with me. Unlike Lesley's hair, Janet had what we called in Brooklyn "kinky Jew hair." Unless you have it, you'd have to be Black to understand what it is.

I rang the bell and Lesley answered looking wonderful. Over her shoulder, towards the back of the living room, I could see an ironing board set up. Janet must be touching up something. She was. Her hair. There she was, in a bra and panties, with her cheek on the ironing board, and an iron in her hand. The last time I was so shocked was the night I learned what a fall was when my date, who had forgotten something upstairs, did a quick turn-around to get it. Her ponytail flipped in my face. Now it gets Freudian. I grabbed it. Now it gets bad. It came off in my hand. Fake hair? Who knew? I stood there, turned to stone. That was in high school. It was a first and last date.

Back to Janet. I didn't really notice the difference, before and after except for an odd, burning smell that lingered for a while. She slipped into a skirt and blouse. The blouse had darts that accentuated her attributes (C'mon folks, I'm trying to keep this book PG). We dated for a while. She taught me, as Dr. Perkins would have said, things I wasn't going to learn in class. I felt badly but the reason I kept dating her was not so much for what I was learning, but for Lesley to answer the knock at the door.

We all know these things end badly. One night, I went to pick up Janet and Lesley did not answer the door. Janet did. By now, I knew what awaited me, so I was only so crestfallen. However, now there was another scene being played out towards the back of the living room. Tonight, Lesley had a date—someone she obviously had been seeing for some time. Had they been any closer together they would have melded into one another, but for one thing. She was average height. Her boyfriend was Paul Bunyan. I was speechless. He wasn't for her, couldn't be for her, was definitely not her type. He actually had on a flannel shirt and had more hair on his face than I did on my head and much more than that on his head, if you could see that high. Then she introduced me, smiling that beaming smile of love in the air. What came out of my mouth—again-- was pure Ralph Kramden—mahumahumahum. What the hell? This was not fair.

I think I was so taken aback that it finally dawned on Janet what was what. The favors stopped coming, again no pun intended. I called Lesley every-so-often in the hopes that she'd come to her senses. I didn't call Janet.

WILLIAM A. GRALNICK

"Nature, like a careful gardener,
thus takes her seeds from a bed of a
particular nature, and drops them
in another . . .

– Elliott Coues, known as the
father of modern ornithology,
graduated from GW's precursor
Columbian University in 1861
and the medical school in 1863

Peanuts, Popcorn, Candy

The mouth I had so hungered for now held a
forked tongue that flicked and spit at me

I never had much luck with girls named after candy. I thought Taffy would be different. I was walking past the auditorium and there was a vision approaching me from a distance. I know you've read that before and think several screws holding my brain in place were lost. Let me describe her; you decide.

She was wearing sneakers and shorts. The legs that joined them were tanned and toned. Her upper body screamed tennis along with several other things. Her face could have been on a magazine cover. Her smile expanded as she approached; her teeth should have been in both a toothpaste commercial and a dentistry commercial. Her hair was pulled back into a ponytail—a ponytail befitting a pony as it swished back and forth by her lower back. I had never seen her on campus before. As she approached me, she totally short-circuited my opening by greeting me with a very engaging, "Hi! I'm Taffy." Could this be possible? Taffy was making the first move on me?

I stopped; so did she. The questions darted back and forth. Where're you from? What are you studying? And so on. She was the most naturally, friendly girl I'd ever met and she was talking to me. The Lord spoke to the people of Israel in many voices. Hearing God in the air, I asked her if she was busy or if she'd like to go get coffee or tea or ice cream or see the monuments or just spend a few hours standing next to me and smiling. We went for coffee, which as it turned out, neither of us drank.

We had tea and a donut and continued to talk. Taffy was from Utah. She wasn't enrolled at GW but at BYU. She was sort of on a mission and was attending a conference at Lisner Auditorium. She'd never been to New York and thought of it as a location in Dante's Inferno. She loved that I was Jewish and had tons of questions to ask me. Now, if you are paying close attention, you are picking up many hints that I as a beauty-blinded fool totally missed.

What kind of mission would such a young woman be on? I asked myself. She explained that she was a Morman and the church required that each member give up a year to go somewhere and bring the grace of God with them. "Oh," I said, "that kind of mission." I had thought maybe she was in the CIA or the Marines. As the minutes turned to hours, she peppered me with polite, and interested questions about Judaism. With equal curiosity I volleyed with questions about Mormonism. She suddenly looked at her watch and said, "Oh dear. I have to run. I'll be late for the seminar." The seminar it turns out was to teach these freshly scrubbed, perfect people how to bring the grace of God to wherever they ended up being sent.

I asked when it ended and if she'd like to have a bite to eat afterwards. Her answer was immediate and affirmative. I was getting pretty close to what I thought heaven might have to offer. I posted myself in front of the auditorium and waited. She was late. I was fidgety. Had she gleaned all she needed and was going to stand me up? But no. Out of the shadows bounded the ponytail. It was attached to her ridiculously perfect form. With it came this perfect apology, "Sometimes even those preaching the gospel talk too much." She was sorry she was late. My enchantment was back in full bloom.

I had picked a local diner for dinner. The smiles continued, along with rubbing of arms, and handholding. We were seated and the endless rounds of questions continued. I was fascinated. "How long will you be on campus? Can I see you again?" "Are you going straight back to Utah?" This was a Mr. Clean version of my trip to Mississippi. She'd be around for a week. She'd love to see me again. But she had a question to ask me that she hoped wouldn't be too personal.

Do you get a sense that the taffy is beginning to melt?

"Yes, of course, ask away. You are so sweet and genuine I can't imagine you asking me something that would be hurtful."

She took both my hands in hers, our arms stretched out across the table. She focused her incredibly blue eyes directly on mine. She smiled that smile that had little stars bouncing off her teeth and said, "Bill, don't you care that you and your future children are going to end up in hell?"

Suddenly, I saw her differently. Her hair held the snakes of Medusa. Her starlight teeth turned black. Lightning bolts flew from those blue eyes. That smooth, silky skin became scaled, and those beautiful legs became those of an ostrich ready to run me down. The mouth I had so hungered for held a forked tongue that flicked and spit at me.

The next six days were Taffy-less.

"The measure of success is not whether you have a tough problem to deal with, but whether it is the same problem you had last year."

– John Foster Dulles, politician, diplomat, eight years as Secretary of State under Dwight Eisenhower, graduated from GW Law in 1911

PART FIVE

Buddy
CAN YOU
SPARE A DIME?

"Some fun was wise and permissible but fun cost money."

Introduction

One of the several pre-leaving for college discussions I was laden with was about money. I had no idea about finances. I was smart enough to know that going to school out of town was more expensive than taking the New York State Scholarship I won and going to school in New York, even if it was out of Brooklyn and upstate somewhere. I also knew that my father's extended illness and loss of six months of work had hit us hard but other than talking about it like someone had died in the family, there were no obvious signs to me that, now back at work, anything had changed. Yet came the talk.

My parents paid for the meal plan. I was expected to use it. I was going to college to learn things not to have fun. Some fun was wise and permissible but fun cost money. And there came the crux of it all. I would be given an allowance of twenty dollars a week. What I did with it was up to me, but since I would be studying and not paying for food, it should be enough. When I was ten, my allowance was ten cents a week. By my pre-teens and early teens, it had jumped to a quarter and then a dollar (with chores attached). I guess twenty bucks was a big deal. Not in the nation's capital, it wasn't.

Most of us had to find a way to supplement our finances. I had a fraternity brother who put himself through school playing poker. I can hardly shuffle a deck of cards. That wouldn't have been it for me. Some worked campus jobs. There were also the cafeteria, White Castle, retail, and of course on The Hill.

I tried a few things. The experiences were as bizarre as they were with girls. Take for instance the place looking for seasonal sales help. It was a wholesale business that only sold to government and diplomatic officials. Credentials were needed to get in. I had never sold anything to anyone in my life. I got the job.

Standing on one's feet all day behind a counter dealing with pretentious, snotty adults sucks. It wasn't long before two things happened. The first was I got sick and tired of the abuse and having to suck it up. The return on investment wasn't great. I was paid minimum wages, got no discount, and almost ended up with "TMJ" (FYI it is a dental term) from clenching my jaws. The second was it wasn't terribly busy, so I ended up spending hours looking at the men's jewelry case over which I stood. In it was a tie tack (they were very in then) that I lusted after. It was black onyx set in burnished eighteen carat gold. Even wholesale the price was not one I could handle. So, one day, I decided to steal it.

Had you read the precursor to the book, *The War of the Itchy Balls and Other Tales from Brooklyn*, you'd know that in elementary school I stole a couple of packs of Topps Baseball cards. I had agita for weeks. They were a nickel a pack. This was grand larceny—not really but compared to Topps baseball cards . . . Every day after this brainstorm I was a wreck planning my heist, going over my get away. The easy part was getting it. Just reach into the cabinet. Tie tacks are not very big, maybe a little smaller than a chickpea. I put it on my tie as if I were trying it on. I wore it the whole day. I guess if anyone noticed, they'd figure it was mine. No one said anything so I walked out with it. I worked a few more days and turned in my notice. I didn't sleep for a week or wear the tie tack for a year.

I answered another ad. This one took me to a spectacular brownstone in upper NW DC. I walked in and noticed that I was the only white face around. I was courteously offered a seat and a cold drink. After a brief wait, I was ushered into an office that was decorated in African. Behind a hand-carved desk sat a very large, black man wearing a very large diamond pinky ring, and a dashiki to cover his very large belly. We had a chat that mostly centered about foreign affairs, a subject of both interest and knowledge of mine. I got the job. Within a week, after orientation, I figured out what the guy did—he was an international arms dealer! Back to the want ads.

Then one day, my roommate came charging in and said, "I GOT US JOBS!" Now come the stories about that job.

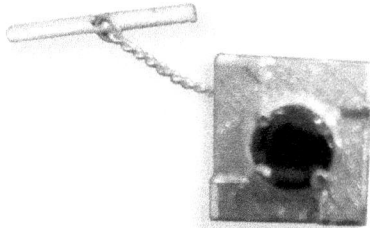

The Siren of Tie Tacks

"People feel like the system is rigged against them. And here's the painful part: they're right. The system is rigged."

– Senator Elizabeth Warren, entered GW on a debate scholarship in 1964, left to marry John Warren in 1968

What passed for protest at GW.

THE *Blind* LEADING
THE *Blind*

"We knew why there was a noticeable color difference marked by a weathered line one third the way up the Washington Monument . . . and so, so much more."

Clearly the nation's capital is a tourist town. In the '60s, there were a few standard ways to see the city. One was by taxi. This is a little shady. The drivers didn't have licenses to guide. The tourist had no idea if what he was being told or even seeing was correct.

Then there were the folks who came in by bus or train and their trip included a licensed guide. Here your experience was governed by time. There were four-hour or eight-hour tours. If you were staying overnight and had a second tour, you got the whole deal, seeing things that most others never got to see.

Then there was the old stand-by. That was the Greyline Bus Tour. Mind you, the Greyline of then is not the Greyline of now. Then most of the guides looked like they were touts fresh from the track. While I'm sure they weren't, they also all seemed small, bald, cigar smokers who would be lucky if they could get up the stairs of the bus no less survive a day in DC's heat and humidity. The driver guides, especially from the Cadillac of that type of company, Tauck Tours, ribbed them mercilessly.

And such was the state of tourist guiding in our nation's capital—until that is a sergeant in the honor guard at the Tomb of the Unknown Soldier came up with an idea. Now understand this was not just a sergeant, although being in that unit conferred upon one a status that had little to touch it, unless you were in the fighting corps—Rangers, Marine, Special Forces/Green Beret. His father was the controlling stockholder in one of the major Hollywood movie companies. So, not only did this sergeant come from money, he came from contacts. When he wanted to do something there was always someone with money and someone else who knew someone else to make it happen. The idea? To create a guide service that would be so different from taxi cabs and hacking, coughing, bus guides in rumpled uniforms, that it would be a standout.

Called Heritage Cavaliers Guide Service, it recruited college age, mostly all college students, from around DC. He put them in a uniform. A green blazer with a breast pocket logo, black pants, black shoes. He created a study guide for the licensing test and held prep classes. The guide was not only learning what was needed for the license but many archival facts that one would not hear on any other tour save one given by someone at the Smithsonian Institute.

We knew where things were that no one ever got taken to like the stunningly simple Franciscan Monastery and knew not only what "indulgences" were but that the monastery was one of only a few places in the world where they could be conferred. We knew the reason why George Washington wanted a National Cathedral but also why by the 1960s, it still hadn't been completed. We knew why there was a noticeable color difference marked by a weathered line one third the way up the Washington Monument, that there was a ghost in the Octagon House and so, so much more. You really got your money's worth. But that wasn't all.

Our boy-genius developed two-day tours. The second day might take you through the Bull Run Battlefield, the Luray Caverns for a touchy-feely learning experience about stalactites and stalagmites, and a run around part of the Shenandoah Valley to see the indescribable fall foliage. Or you might go the other way, following parts of the Underground Railroad and up to Harper's Ferry.

There was a hitch. Most of us didn't have cars. A few more puffs of smoke from the ears and out came the idea to sign contracts with companies like Tauck. We'd board the bus in the morning and take the mike for the day. At first, the drivers didn't like giving up the mike nor did they like us. In us, they saw their obsolescence and a drop in their tips. But soon the word spread. It was a helluva lot easier to drive and not have to talk and point, and even more importantly, we drew much better tips ("had to pay for college" or many another sad song the drivers couldn't sing) and of course split with them. Within a year they loved us, and we had trouble filling the billings.

That became even worse because the Einstein of the tourist business was gushing with brilliant ideas. He began advertising to schools that had senior class trips to DC. (Who would you trust your students with—a bus driver or a uniformed, clean cut etc. etc. etc.?) And there was more. What about those foreign visitors? Soon we were doing eight-hour gigs in French, Spanish, Italian, and Portuguese. And if one of us, like me, had the misfortune of being able to stumble his way through an eight-hour tour in two languages . . . well let me tell you, those days brought the worst headaches I to this day ever had.

Nor was he finished. What about all those high-end pols and diplomats who needed chauffeuring to this watering hole or that? Not only were we a lot cheaper than the standard limo companies, the government provided the cars and because we were guides, we knew our way around the city (no GPS). This stroke of genius brings us to four memorable stories: the African who hated red lights, the A I got on a test taken the morning after I had been up all night with a fly-on-the-wall perspective on exactly the issue the test was on, the King and I, a brush with southern style, old-fashioned religion, and the discovery that a cemetery is the worst place to drop dead.

Take a breath, turn the page, and grab some Visine.

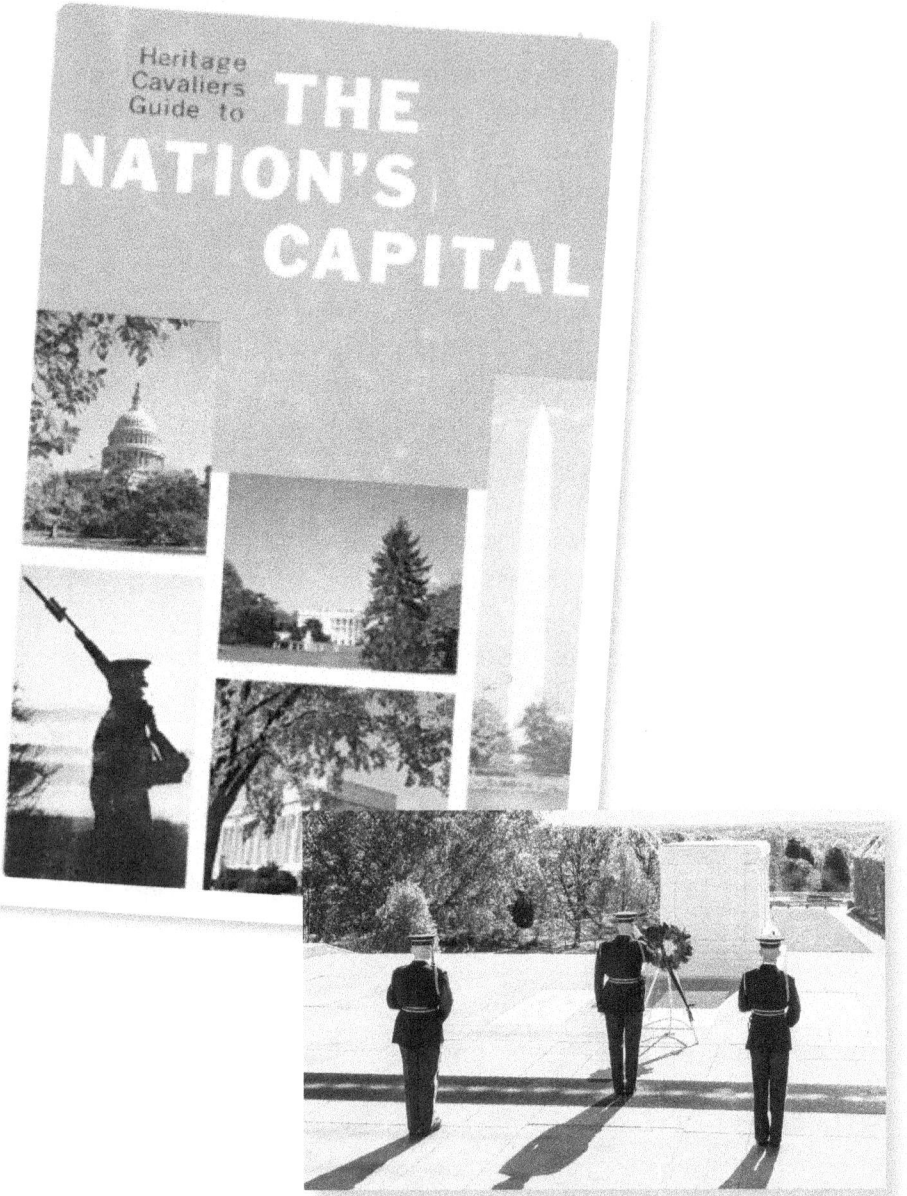

Iconic reverence.

HE DIDN'T HAVE
TO TAKE

Burial

SO LITERALLY

He was a corpulent gent in his '50s with a wife who made the couple look like they'd stepped out of the Jack Spratt story.

One of the worst places to die is in a cemetery. Take my word for it.

It was a hot, humid summer's day (are there any other kinds?) in Washington, DC. It was a day where nobody wanted to move, no less move quickly. One of the things to know about bus tours is that they are scheduled and scheduled for pretty good reasons. The driver may have another tour after this one, or he's been driving several days before he got to you and by law has to stop driving at a certain time, some visitations have tickets for certain times. If you're late your group could be held back, or worse, it could be packed together with the group that was on time and instead of a tour group you became a herd. There were also attractions that started at certain times—exactly at certain times. You missed the time you stood in the back and couldn't see anything. Also, the experienced drivers knew that just five minutes early or late meant being able to park the bus in a spot that made getting a good standing place for the group a cinch—or not.

All of this is a run up to the 11:00 a.m. changing of the guard at the Tomb of the Unknown Soldier this hot, humid DC morning for which we were about to be late. The bus was a tour group from Spain, some singles, mostly women above fifty and the rest, husbands, wives, and children. If you were putting together a group for compatibility, this would not have been it. The driver did his job. Then I had to do mine, which resembled shepherding. We were all set for the "sight."

And some sight it is. Every hour, except after midnight when it is every two hours, there is a highly ritualistic changing of the guard. It is precision dancing in slow motion that involved rifles and the exchanging of them while the ritual is taking place. The only thing I know of that comes close is watching the seemingly paralyzed guards at Buckingham Palace. Up the hill, off to the left a-ways, is JFK's eternal flame. In sum, it is holy ground. There's an old Brooklyn expression used when something is so good, "It's to die for." Regrettably, one of my group took it literally.

As I said, time was of the essence and Spain, and most of western Europe, has a little "manana" in it. It's like everyone takes a bit of valium before the day begins, moves through the morning at a leisurely pace, makes it to lunch, and then takes a nap. Definitely not the American way. This group started its day late and managed to lose more time at every stop. It got to the point where I was seriously considering leaving without someone just to make the point in a universal language. But I didn't, which was too bad.

One of the Mr. Tardies was a corpulent gent in his '50s with a wife who made the couple look like they'd stepped out of the Jack Spratt story. In tow, there were two, not surprisingly on the way to being corpulent, children. Around middle school age was one, late elementary school the other. I had stressed the logistics of the guard changing 'til I was blue in the face. I exacted promises from all to be on the bus when I said they had to. They lied.

When your bus doesn't have a primo spot, it not only is going to greatly slow your ability to get out of the area quickly, worse it meant somewhat of a pitched hike up to the tomb. If you were in the back, and short to boot, you mostly saw nothing. Nipping at their heels, I tried to move them up the hill, weaving this way and that, as spaces opened up or I blithely opened them up with a little push here an "excuse me" there, so my people could see what they came to see. Too bad for those I elbowed out of the way. This is the stuff of which good tips are made. There was some grumbling. Remember we were doing all of this in a sauna bath. People were sweating like pigs. (You should excuse me, but do pigs sweat?). The men had shed their sport jackets: their shirts were sopping wet. Like a battle commander, I urged them on. And we made it. The grumbling stopped and like the sun, their smiles got brighter.

As we turned to head back to the bus, I heard someone scream. This was followed by a great commotion. In several languages, I distinctly heard, "Someone get a doctor!!" I did a smart one-eighty, to see Mr. Corpulent flat, well not really flat, but lying on the ground face down. He hadn't tripped. He had had heat stroke and then a heart attack and fell like a giant sequoia.

Getting a doctor and medical equipment in a cemetery could be part of a bad joke. After all, everyone is already dead. I told my charges to stay put and ran down the hill to a path hoping to find a military patrol. I didn't. I picked a direction and ran. I was exuding sweat like I'd become a waterfall. I had sweated through everything—shirt, underwear, pants. There was so much sweat in my shoes that my feet were sliding around in them making squishy sounds. Finally—a patrol jeep. I wheezed out the problem, he got on his handset, told me to hop in, wheeled around, and raced back to the tomb where we'd meet an ambulance and now two dead bodies, one figurative (me).

The medical team did not pronounce him on the spot. That was sensible. They gave him oxygen, loaded him in the ambulance, someone followed with the family, and officially he wasn't dead until he arrived at George Washington Hospital. What did I do? You've heard the expression, "The show must go on?" It was now noon and they'd paid for another four hours. Strangely enough, they wanted it, so I gave it to them—a very strange four hours, especially when at lunch someone called the hospital to find out neither he nor the family would be making the rest of the tour. In fact, they were arranging for the body to be shipped back to Spain. But the show went on.

I should mention that I was extraordinarily well-tipped for the day. I also should mention that I went to pay a condolence call on the wife and children.

Finally, I should mention that I then went to a bar and had several snootfuls.

"I think I fulfill a very funny Indian stereotype because I love technology."

– Manish Dayal, actor, CW
breakout role in *The Hundred Foot Journey*, graduated
with an International Business
degree in 1964

Your tour escort at your service.

Beautiful Bermuda

What could go wrong? Then we had the trip orientation.

Bermuda is a gem. The waters glisten. The island is lovely, its people even nicer. Best yet, if you live on the east coast, it's very easy to get to, especially from the mid-Atlantic states. It was cause for another brainstorm by our chief Cavalier. Why not try to be a real travel agent? Instead of going after groups, why not put one together? An ad runs targeting young working adults and don't you know, it works. About twenty folks signed up. Magically, they were fairly evenly split male to female roughly all in the late '20s. What could go wrong? At first seemingly nothing. Then we had the trip orientation.

Presenting herself as a cowgirl from Texas was this blond who was really a cowgirl from Texas. She was tall, broad-shouldered, with hair that had that Clairol flair. She had a Playboy figure, and an accent you could cut with a barbecue rib knife. As she walked into the room, all the men's eyes popped right out of their heads and rolled down to their chests, probably the better to see hers. As for the girls, a look of "oh shit" crossed all their faces, none of which were terribly pretty nor much of anything special, especially in contrast to Miss Mickey Gilley of 1964. That's not true but for sure as a model she had amassed a shelf full of Miss This's and That's probably starting at birth.

The boss had chosen four of his top people to accompany the trip. He was more concerned with rave reviews than making a profit. There's a big difference between guiding a tour group in a town full of internationally famous tourist attractions and guiding a group of single souls on a small island that had few attractions, after you left the beach. One of them was Devil's Hole, a very deep, natural hole in the ground filled with water and fish. You could rent motor bikes and self-tour yourself around, but mostly you stayed at the pool and drank or on the beach and got sunburned while drinking.

The major difference in this type of endeavor is that each person thinks you are there just for them. Instead of moving a group on a bus and then herding them along like a flock, this was like herding cats, each with a distinct sense of where it wanted to go that was often not where you wanted it to go. And when not enough attention was thought to be given, you were the target. So, what could go wrong? Let me count the ways:

- Flight was late taking off and arriving.
- Transportation pick-up was late, uncomfortable, and had air-conditioning problems.
- Miss Galveston was such an unbelievable sight in a bikini that the guys were drawn to her like bits of steel to a magnet, bits that she demurely brushed off. This made the other girls not want to be at the pool.
- A chain could come off a mini-bike and its rider had the perfect but mistaken confidence that you could put it back on—quickly.
- Someone could fall off a bike and end up with such road rash that it would last long after the trip—bad publicity.
- And the worst of all, one of the guides began to get hit on by Miss Texas Two-Step and instead of following the rules, which made that an absolute no-no, he would discreetly encourage her. That was me.

The good news was that the trip didn't end like the one to Arlington National Cemetery. Not everyone was thrilled, but they all arrived home alive. It wasn't until then that I learned that Miss Distraction of Abilene was a stewardess and had an apartment, just a few miles from where I lived. And that's where the story begins. It is a long, short story.

We had a few phone calls. Talking to her on the phone was like having PG-17 phone sex. The breathless drawl was worse than fantasy because you knew this girl was real, alive, and nearby.

Finally, the invitation came. I turned into the Road Runner and was there in record time. She was dressed to kill, kill in the sense that seeing how little she had on, some of which was see-through, that you could walk in the door, have a heart attack and drop dead. It worsened when she asked my approval of what she had chosen for the night, doing slow turns this way and that. She handed me a beer—from Texas, and later hard stuff. The next thing I knew, we were not headed out but were in her very large, very soft bed. I'm not sure how we got there. I was still clothed, and she was in her bra and panties. Forget a sight for sore eyes. I don't have the cliché for what I was seeing. She slowly unhaberdashed me down to her state of undress and then . . . began to talk. And did she have a list of topics, enough so that I began to realize that she had scripted this play and acted in it many times.

Then came the *coup de gras*. The phone rang. Thirty minutes she talked. The chatter was interspersed with "of course, honeys and you know I do, honeys and I can't wait to see you, honeys, and yes, I love you, honeys." She got off the phone and apologized with this. "I'm sorry, honey but that was my fiancé, he's on active duty and we don't get to talk a lot. I hope you don't mind."

Flumoxed, I was rehaberdashed, kissed good night, and shown the door.

And that too is "da troot!"

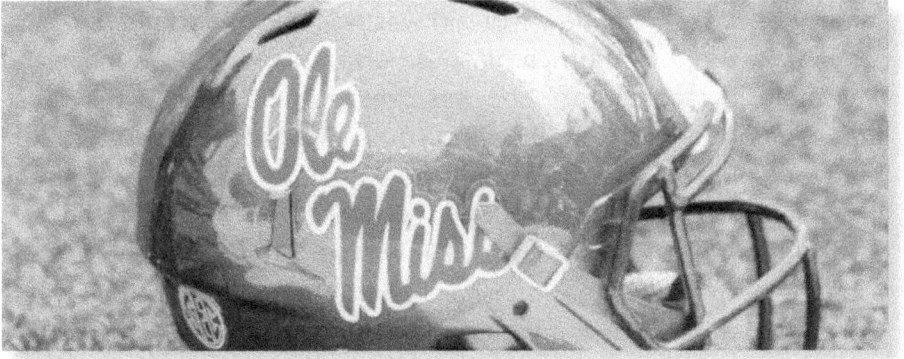

Speaks for itself . . .

Forbidden Love

AT FIRST SIGHT

"The French call it a coup de foudre—a clap of thunder."

The out of the country tour idea didn't turn out so well but the boss had a winner in high school trips. What better thing to offer than a civics cum history lesson on wheels, with meals, and right in the middle of the material being presented.

Our first trip came from a high school deep in Mississippi. It was the *crème de la crème* or whatever that is in Mississippi. The mayor's son, the preacher's daughter, the children of the agro-kings and industrial Mighty Mouses and, of course, the most trustworthy teachers, four of them to watch this moving mass of hormones 24-7. That's foreshadowing. I probably was the biggest problem, but let's not start with it.

I got a call at three a.m. from the group's hotel. I needed to get there pronto. The trip would be down two participants. It seems that the preacher's daughter, who was beautiful enough that many a Bible personality would have loved dreaming about her, and the Mr. Quarterback, All-Everything, the principal's son, had slipped their hobbles and managed to get the two of themselves into one bed. One of the teachers was doing a bed check and opened the door. I'll put it this way. What she saw was her career coming to a crashing end and the need for her and her family to move out of town. The kids, both probably sporting Scarlet Letters, were on the next plane out to Jackson, of Mr. and Mrs. Johnny Cash fame.

Now me. The kids came tumbling off the plane looking like they'd fallen out of a washer/dryer. A quick vote mandated that the first stop would be the hotel. When they came tumbling out of the elevator, they looked quite different, especially Ann Black. I would say she was more than a match for Lorelai and added to that package was a Mississippi drawl. Listening to her talk was like watching honey flow out of a jar. I was dumbstruck. The French call it a *coup de foudre*—a clap of thunder. Apparently, there was reciprocity.

At every stop was the opportunity to take her hand and help her from the bus. There was every opportunity to brush shoulders. At sites with railings, there was every opportunity to slip into line before or after her and either slide my hand up so that it touched hers or vice versa. When that happened, sparks of electricity shot up and down the guiderails though no one else seemed to be shocked by them. While I had to visit every lunch and dinner table, I seemed to find a way to leave hers 'til last and spend the most amount of time there. An empty chair magically was always the one next to her. I was bewitched.

This is day one-and-a-half of a seven-day trip. Somehow, the teachers were either unconcerned or didn't notice, though that can't be said for Ann's classmates. The twittering (that was teenage communication before Twitter) was incessant. Every hour seemed doubled or tripled in length. At times, I wasn't guiding or we were taking a break, Ann and I began to talk. She came from a small town outside Jackson, Barnesville. Her daddy, as she called him, was a gentleman farmer and did well. Ann did well in school, was a bible-believing Southern Methodist, a cheerleader, Miss Everything It Was Possible to Be in Barnesville. She applied and was accepted to U. Miss in Jackson.

I gave her the same tour of me. She was fascinated, like she was listening to stories from another planet. She'd never met a Jew before but she knew that Jesus was one. I wouldn't say Ann was the brightest bulb in the package but looks, good breeding, long, honey blond hair (have you noticed yet, I seemed to have a type), and that accent—it made up for a lot of other missing pieces. Probably all of them.

Every day was the same but for the advancing of lightning bolt sets of touching, leaning, "oh let me get that leaf out of your hair" moments. In a way, it was like taking the long walk to the electric chair. You were treated very well but the end was inevitable—but for one thing. The warden doesn't kiss you. On the last day, Ann found a secluded spot during a downtime moment, turned me around and kissed me full on the lips. For days, I had to wear braces on my legs because they had turned to Jell-O.

As she boarded the bus, she politely shook my hand, said thank you, and in the process slipped her name, address, and phone number into my palm. "Call me" the note said. I have A-fib now. It is good I didn't have it then.

So, I did and that accent, now coming through the phone was even more devastating. The "do you remembers" from the trip, whispered into the phone made them seem like they were pornographic scenes rather than the simple, growing hormonal response every teenage boy gets when something brings on that *coup de foudre*. We did this and wrote through the fall. I was a college man and she was on her way to wowing everyone at Ole Miss. One night on the phone, she told me breathlessly of the coming Ole Miss/Mississippi State game. Would I come? She would take care of the arrangements, I just had to get there.

On Thursday, I boarded the Greyhound to Jackson. Aside from the crushingly, boring ride, I remember just a few things. One was the clientele—read a Faulkner novel. One was at a rest stop where I walked into the men's room not noticing the "colored only" sign, did the same thing with the water fountain, and then looked up to see the whole bus station staring at me with hate in their eyes. The light dawned. To pass the time away, I had brought Woody Allen's latest book. I could not stop giggling, creating more stares and laughing to myself, knowing that no one around me would understand one story in it. Corned beef? Mayonnaise? White bread . . . not a chance.

Finally, we rolled into the Jackson bus station, I looked down and there she was. But something had happened. She didn't look quite the same, not at all bad, but somehow a little fuller, a little less cute, a tiny bit undone. I didn't know . . . something. I chalked it up to the infernally, long, bus ride. But not only Ann was there. Her party in waiting was there to greet me. She quickly pointed to one and said, "Take his suitcase up to the room." And he did.

She then grabbed me by the hand and pulled me off to the bar. The only other time in my life that I was as unnerved in a bar like this was when I was in a German beer drinking club with about 700 drunk Germans. There were Confederate flags everywhere, every other song was "Dixie," kids said "nigger" as many times in a sentence as did northern teens said, "like." The artwork was a gallery whose works leaned heavily into the genre of Confederate generals and gorgeous plantations. Now, it was I who seemed transported to another planet.

My observations were broken by Ann introducing me to Farmer John. Stereotype? You bet. Mop of hair that defied combing, white t-shirt (white because it hadn't gotten enough beer and tobacco juice on it to have changed color), overhauls that stretched over the broadest shoulders I'd ever seen, a beard that would have challenged a John Deere. They say stripes make you look thinner. These did nothing for his prodigious belly. He wore white socks and black shoes. He slapped me on the back, which I hate, said "Welcome to Ole Miss." You must be the Jew-boy Annie here's been palaverin' about since last summer." I drew myself up to my full height, prepared to take my last breath, and mumbled, "I am."

About the game, I remember nothing except that overwhelming sense that I was in the wrong place. There wasn't too much interaction between Ann and me but for hand-holding, because I felt like 70,000 screaming farmers were screaming at us. It was the next night, my last that it all came to a head.

Ann asked me if I had ever been to a drive-in movie. I had not. She had a car. In Mississippi, I think you can drive at eight or nine. Off we went to see I know not what and don't to this day. Once we got parked, gotten some drinks and settled in, the best expression for what happened next would be that she jumped me. I thought she was going to push my lips to the back of my neck. I thought if her tongue had a hook on it, when retracted it would come back up with some part of my intestines attached to it. There was squirming, and moaning, grabbing and pulling, grunting and snorting. At one point, I looked up and could not see through the windows, that's how fogged they had become. It was a cool night outside the car and a hot night in it.

All this turned out to be was a prelude and not to what you think and every good ole boy would hope. It was a prelude to a breathless conversation, almost a plea, as she proposed to me. Yes, that's what it says.

"Oh Bill, let's get married. Daddy (there it was again) has lots of room and lots of buildings on his farm. We could finish school here." And (roll the drums please), "I don't care if you're a Jew. I'll pray for our babies every day of their lives." When you are in a fog-laden car, inextricably intertwined with another person, parking in a drive-in lot where you don't know where any road goes in any direction, it is hard to plot an escape—or think of a response.

I have no idea what I said. I said a lot. None of the words were, "yes" or "great idea, my folks would love that." The next day as I boarded the bus with a hopeful kiss goodbye from Ann, I was thrilled to be getting into my time capsule and returning to my part of the galaxy.

There's more.

We did write a few times more. I did get another invitation. I declined it. I'm not sure how it came about; I think through some correspondence I had with the teachers who were on last year's tour. Word had it that Ann had fallen head over heels for a navy man who was on leave in Jackson. She gave her all to him and it seems it had let us call it a lasting impact. This I pondered could have been why she looked ever so slightly different to me when I arrived those many months later.

Thus, before her daddy and momma killed or exiled her, she needed a wedding. She fell for me. I was in the right place at the right time and thus had the target placed on my chest.

In my next book you'll meet the girl who had already had the baby, but for now, I would understand if you were muttering to yourself, "What the hell is the matter with that boy?!?"

Frankly, at that time, I couldn't have given you an answer.

The Diplomat

WHO WOULD BE

King Maker

"The Cabots speak only to the Lodges . . .
the Lodges speak only to God."

Sometimes when you're in the middle of something unusual, the kind of thing that most nineteen year olds wouldn't have a shot at being involved in, you step back and wonder, "How did I get into this?" Again, it started with a phone call.

My boss needed me to drive the United States Ambassador to South Vietnam, Henry Cabot Lodge, to a meeting. I protested. "But, but, but," I stammered, "my final is tomorrow morning at eight a.m." "In what?" he asked. "Southeast Asian Politics," said I. "Dummy," he retorted, "this is the Ambassador to South Vietnam. You should pay me to give you this job!"

Not thinking about the likelihood of someone speaking to me at all no less about international diplomacy who came from a family about whom it was said, "The Cabots speak only to the Lodges, and the Lodges speak only to God," I took the job. It turned out the Lodges also spoke to at least one Gralnick, but we're a long way from there.

You political junkies will remember that the Republican party was in a period of self-immolation, ironically sort of like now. Should they reach far to the left and choose New York State Governor Nelson Rockefeller as their nominee or even further to the right and nominate Arizona Senator Barry Goldwater. The men hated one another and so did their followers. Sound familiar? It was decided by Republican peacemaker and oracle, Joseph Alsop, that he would open his house in Georgetown for a smoking of the peace pipe meeting from which would come the unity to run a presidential campaign. High on the list was Cabot-talker, Henry Cabot Lodge. I picked up him and his wife at the appointed time and place and treated them with the deference they were due, or at least expected. The evening got off to a nice start with a little small talk.

Then the talk turned to the evening and turned from English to French. Something told me the ethical thing to do was to tell them that I understood almost every word they were saying. I was right. They were appreciative. Back we went to English. The Ambassador asked me a few questions about my studies, and I told him about my final now about twelve hours away for which I was not studying. He said, "Tell you what. Whenever I'm not talking to someone else you ask me any questions you can think of and I'll answer them for you. Feel free to quote me."

Holy South Vietnam, Batman!

I had hit the jackpot.

Lodge was true to his word. But before we get there, there was more jackpot for this political science student to see—politics in action. There were real politicians, right off the front pages of the newspapers, grabbing others by the lapels; there were real arguments. Name-calling and cursing abounded. Rockefeller, who had a reputation for being a different human being with a bunch of 80 proof in him, was a wildman. He got so angry at someone his face turned crimson. He bolted out the door forgetting that it opened onto a small, banistered porch where, in order to get to the street, you had to make a left and walk down the stairs. He didn't stop, hit the banister at belt height and were it not for his relatively new bride known to all as "Happy" who grabbed him by the belt, one can only imagine the picture that would have been on the front pages of America's papers. As it was, Happy seemed not to be.

Meanwhile, back at the ranch, the Lodge's decided to leave and my limo education continued. The next morning in my "blue book" there was hardly an essay that didn't quote Henry Cabot Lodge "who said to me at a party last night . . ." Or some variation thereof.

I dropped Lodge off well after midnight and was stunned that he didn't tip me. He saw the look on my face and said, "The tip is included in the fee I paid." I said, "No Sir, it isn't." Unfortunately, the slamming of the bulletproof doors kept that sentence caged in the car.

I did however ace the final and get an A in the course. I needed that more than the sawbuck I was expecting.

ANOTHER

Short Story

WITH A

Long History

At least I didn't end up like Adnan Khashoggi

My boss was excitable and enthusiastic. It was hard to imagine he spent long hours marching impeccable strides in the heat of the day or the chill of night guarding the Tomb of the Unknown Soldier. That was a lifetime ago and now he was retired. His father had left him zillions in stock. That's certainly enough to get one excited.

On this particular call, he was very excited. He had gotten a call from the Department of State. The King of Saudi Arabia was in town and needed a limo driver. Not everyone gets to drive the King, so the boss man told me there was a lot riding on this in terms of future possibilities. What could I say? I'd shower, shave, put on my uniform, and treat him like a king. I was given the particulars and set about getting ready.

The phone rang again. This time it was a much more muted

boss, struggling with his words, pouring out the "I'm sorrys, the I never thought abouts . . . it's, it's my faults, . . . the I'll make it up to you."

Like I said, not everyone gets to drive the King. They did a background check, saw that I was Jewish, and someone else got to drive the King.

Ya can't win 'em all. At least I didn't end up like Adnan Khashoggi.

And you know, I wasn't that upset. It wasn't the first time anti-Semitism and I had run into one another, nor would it be the last. I knew that for sure. Clearly, Kings don't tip. And I understand most of them, except the ones on chess boards, are not happy, go-lucky, I'd love to have a drink with you kinds of guys. I said to myself, "Who needs that?" I had a great story to tell and in minutes I was in a bar telling it.

WILLIAM A. GRALNICK

"The only way there is to know God is through what he calls the 'proof of existence' (al-burhan al-wujadt), which is a direct act of intuition and which does not admit any separation between the knower and the known."

– Ibrahim Kalin, controversial author, poet, philosopher, Islamic scholar, diplomat, special advisor to the president of Turkey, received his PhD from GW in 2004

PART SIX

NOT *Every* ENDING *is* *The End*

College can take a toll on its students.

Introduction

I was coasting until I (or my father) wasn't.

My senior year was a breeze. Because I had graduated from high school with nine college credits that GW accepted, I was almost bored—almost. I had classes two days a week and made a pretty penny guiding. I was coasting 'til graduation day. And why should graduation be any different? I was coasting until I (or my father) hit a proverbial rock.

The Original Polaroid

Mama

DON'T TAKE MY

Kodachrome

AWAY

"It had within its innards a photography lab."

With apologies to Simon and Garfunkel, this is a story about a Polaroid. We must start with the truism, "There are some mistakes you only get to make once." This is a story about one of them.

Just before my graduation from college, the Polaroid camera was being produced for the mass market. They were big, heavy, tricky to use—and expensive. My mother bought one for my father. I'm not sure why. I don't ever remember seeing him with a camera in his hands that wasn't photographing someone's teeth. He was a dentist. Maybe she thought this would get him to take more than dental pictures. I really don't know. I do know mama took the Kodachrome away and the Polaroid was on the packing list for graduation day at The George Washington University.

It is reasonable that a Polaroid should be the winner in the

Gralnick the camera-for-the-graduation sweepstakes. After all, it had within its innards a photography lab. It took a picture, developed the picture and then handed it to you. Well, not quite on that last part. At the end of camera, set in a smart leather case, was a little door. You flipped it open to expose the lip of the roll of film. This you grabbed, pulled it out, and tore it off. That set the next space on the roll to become a picture. It was pretty magical.

The picture was snapped and developed itself in I believe sixty seconds. Too little time and it was underexposed. Too long and it came out too dark. So, like he used his watch to time x-rays, my dad timed the pictures. At the appointed moment, one was instructed to pull the picture out and watch it begin to go from this grey mass into a black and white picture. Pretty cool.

Here's the scene. Graduates are lined up between two buildings and parade through the center of campus called the Quadrangle, going to our seats. Our parade passed the lines of leaning parents breathlessly waiting, not-so-nicely elbowing, for that moment when their loved one would come by with a tag attached to his/her tassels that said, "Paid in full." Just kidding. At that precise moment, they could take the multi-thousand-dollar in tuition picture. My mom in seat two seemed to be maneuvering my father by remote control into the perfect shooting angle repeating camera instructions in his ear.

We began our perp walk. He snapped. He flipped open the camera door. I came into sight. He clicked. He grabbed the film. I approached and he pulled—and the entire roll of film came out of the door hanging from his hand looking like a piece of fly paper. If you looked up "crestfallen" in the dictionary there would have been the face of my father.

Fortunately, my roommate's father, who had the basic Brownie camera that had been in production longer than I had been alive, roll of film in it, a wheel on the top to advance it, and a Kodak shop on the corner to develop it saw what happened. He jumped in front of my father and snapped a shot just before it would have been a picture of my back instead of my front.

Glory be to simplicity. There is one graduation picture of me, but I guess that's all one needs. And the Polaroid? I have both the album upon which Simon and Garfunkel single "Kodachrome" is sung and the actual camera, which I hope close to its fifty-fifth birthday will someday be worth something more than the aggravation it gave my parents.

WILLIAM A. GRALNICK

On his criticisms of POLITICO:

"Your writing was so bad it was easy."

> – Senator Harry Reid, lifelong
> politician, youngest ever
> lieutenant governor of Nevada,
> member of the US House of
> Representatives and majority
> leader of the Senate, received
> his JD from GW Law in 1964

"Fecal Midas"

> – Rick Wilson, sharp-tongued
> Republican, anti-Trump political
> commentator, graduated from
> GW 1980

I'm Not Bernie

"That's what my sign said."

Comes my senior year and it seemed logical to continue on for my Master's degree. It wasn't so much my parent's none-too-subtle fear of the draft and Vietnam as it was the expectation that ran in my family, the expectation of still higher education. Here's a tale, true as the others, which will show that life after college didn't change much. It changed so little that it will be the *forschpice* (appetizer) for the third and final book in this series. It will be called, *That's Why They Call It Work.*

Registering for my master's was a shock. On the one hand, it was a lot easier than undergrad, because there were so many fewer students. On the other hand, my first trip to the bookstore almost produced a hernia. I would read more books in my first semester than I had in my entire four years of undergrad. I don't know what was more intimidating, the thought of carrying them home or the thought of reading them. (Remember, no iPads.)

Home was a shock too. I had become friends with friends of my roommate, and I was invited to join them to make up, if I recall, the fifth roommate in a sprawling house in Alexandria, Virginia. In those days, most of Alexandria was almost country. It was past being

239

suburban but not quite the Styx. There are only two of the crew that I remember with any detail and the third, attached so to speak to one of the two who didn't live there or, better said, didn't have her own room there. The one, whose name I don't remember had invented what he said was the first computer match dating service in America. (In the next book you'll read about one of those dates.) The other was Bernie whose attachment was Nancy and there lies the story.

Being the only student in a house of non-students is hard enough. On some days, after four years of college, just being a graduate student is hard enough. On the weekends when no one else faced presenting on a Monday morning a class assignment, the weekends didn't seem to be as much fun as they were as an upper classman in undergraduate school. There were days, and nights, I wished I was an every-day-guy workin' nine to five, with my nights to do with what I wanted.

Meet Bernie, my role model for this pseudo-fantasy.

Bernie was a Polish ditch-digger, literally. He dug ditches for the county not repaired lines a la Glen Campbell. He had two responsibilities in the morning. He had to get up and he had to eat. He didn't even have to remember his shovel. It was provided on the worksite. At five, the whistle blew (actually I don't know if it did or not) and by six p.m. he was out of the shower, in his bath towel, and the sound of popping beer can tops were echoing through the house. On an occasional weeknight but mostly weekends would come Nancy.

As much as Bernie looked like a Polish ditch-digger replete with beer belly is as much as Nancy didn't look like she would be the girlfriend of a Polish ditch digger. She was tall, lithe, beautifully proportioned, dressed to kill, sported long, blond hair, and spoke with what was unmistakably an English accent she had learned from not from being English but listening to and imitating people who were. Bernie sounded nothing like that. I often mused about the attraction. It certainly wasn't his cologne. By the fifth or sixth beer for Bernie there was no Old Spice product that could out duel his body's odor, which was unmistakably that of a brewery—Pabst Blue Ribbon, if I recall correctly. Eventually, I figured it out, but we'll just accept the attraction and go on.

Like the Klopman diamond of Jewish joke fame, Nancy came with a curse. It was not Mr. Klopman, it was Mr. Giancarlo (maybe) of the Mafia (definitely). Nancy had a nose for the good stuff. Bernie could and did satisfy her physical needs and a place where she could be relaxed and not on display. To get the accessories to go with the outfits, and actually the outfits themselves, Bernie would not do. How she met the gentleman (ahem . . .) who was thirty or more years her senior, I don't know. What he did for a living was rumored to be to create death. That apparently required a lot of travel and travel days were Bernie days—and nights.

Assignments in any job often go astray. Scheduling mistakes are made. People aren't where they are supposed to be. The "paperwork" necessary for the job doesn't show up. And so, it was a week when Mr. Senior Citizen showed up unexpectedly in Arlington instead of wherever. He was happy until of course he discovered no one was home.

Now there are certain people and groups of people who have a knack for finding others. It was a Saturday night, we were having a small party, and we noticed some very large men looking in the various windows of the house. Let's make that some very, very large men. Nancy uttered something that shouldn't go in a PG book and suddenly four guys began a simultaneous sweat. The fifth was Bernie and he was too drunk to care and also big enough to hold his own with anyone he could get his hands on—no better than an even bet at that point in the night. In short order, the mission seemed accomplished because like large, Italian ghosts they disappeared as quickly and silently as they had showed up. The phone rang and Nancy departed.

She showed up again mid-week sporting a shiner and explained that her comings and goings would be from now on a lot more tightly restricted. But there was always the *Call of the Wild*. One is sixty, one is twenty-eight. One had mucho body fat, one had none. One is fit as an Olympic swimmer and one well isn't. And the winner is . . . ?

The next Saturday we had no party, but Nancy was over, cooked us all dinner, and sat around drowning in our replay of what had happened while we imbibed a variety of liquids that had alcohol content. The phone rang. Nancy turned as white as a sheet of typing paper. The message typed on the paper said, Mr. Mucho Body Fat was hunting her. He never planned to go away that weekend and we were all in for a "lesson." It seems Nancy was as well-liked in her other crowd as she was in ours. One of her admirers probably took his life in his hands (literally) and tipped her off. She scooted from the house like a mouse that had seen a cat. We continued to drink—copiously.

Then it dawned on us. The killer (and I don't mean Jerry Lee Lewis) would think from last week's reconnaissance reports that she was at our place. They would come looking for Nancy and Bernie and we'd become collateral damage. Children and drunks do the damnedest things. We were both. Expecting at some point to see those same friendly faces in the windows, you'd think we too would take off. We didn't. What we did do was embarrassing.

We began making costumes from things left over from a Halloween party. And signs, don't forget the signs. The letters had to be large, very large, readable through the windows, large. Mine said, "I AM NOT BERNIE—I AM A COW." I kid you not.

The next morning came the good news and the bad news. The good news was having taken a quick inventory we were all alive. The bad news was I had a headache about which they make television commercials.

And Nancy with the laughing, if black and blue, eyes? We never saw her again though on an occasional night home, Bernie would let us know they had figured out their own plan.

We figured we'd keep the signs and costumes—just in case.

This is . . .
The End

"If people can see Earth from up here, see it without those borders, see it without any differences in race or religion, they would have a completely different perspective. Because when you see it from that angle, you cannot think of your home or your country. All you can see is one Earth . . ."

– Anousheh Ansari, Iranian scientist, first Iranian woman in space, first self-funded space tourist to the International Space Station, earned MS in electrical engineering from GW

No explanation needed.

PART SEVEN

The Beginning

Introduction

When my children were old enough to work, they would oft-times complain to me how hard it was. I had two replies. One was, "You didn't believe me when I told you school was the easy part" and more succinctly, "That's why they call it work." The latter has stuck with me and is the title of the third and final book in this memoir series.

It will pick up with getting my first job, landing in Johnstown, Pa., where my track record of pitfalls continued unabated as did encounters I never could have imagined. Curious?

My job, paying the handsome sum of $9,500 came with a country club membership. My first Sunday in town, one of my board members called to ask which church I belonged to and could he give me a ride. Explaining I was Jewish, I heard nothing but silence. Then, "Hmmmm, that's a problem. The country club you get a membership in—well it doesn't take Jews." Ba da boom.

Or being a guest for lunch at that very club with the president of the biggest savings bank in town and being in the middle of this. I was in front, the banker behind me, and behind him a very agitated man. I should add there was a terrific recession and the bank was foreclosing on houses faster than you could say, "Johnny close the door." It seems Mr. Agitation's house was amongst them. The repartee was short and pithy. He said to the banker, "I hope I live long enough to piss on your grave." I would have been shocked if I had time. Came an instant retort, "I hope you don't mind standing in line." We then proceeded to lunch.

I was an attendee at a celebratory dinner for the oldest living graduate of Harvard Law School. This ancient son of the civil war known to believe that after ninety one got the privilege of pinching any woman's ass you wanted, peppered his speech with "Nigra this" and "Nigra that." It didn't take long before a plate dropped somewhere, and then another, and then several more. It was like the all black wait staff was playing the ending of the 1812 Overture with plates, not instruments. It truly was one of the most unusual protest demonstrations I'd ever been witness to.

That was Georgia. In Colorado, I was introduced to the concept of intelligence, not in people's heads but the kind private eyes do. My employers knew more about me than my mother did and were quick to let me know that. It was the land of Coors beer where the head of the poli sci department at the university was quoted as saying, "I don't care who runs this town, I'm from St. Louis and I'm tellin' you, you can't make good tasting beer from clean water." A clear and dangerous slap at the Coors family.

In many ways, besides kids riding their horses to class, I would learn that the West is different from the East.

My next trip was taken in a car that had a singular problem. If you turned it off, it wouldn't start again. I drove several days and 1800 miles without ever turning off the car. Now aren't you intrigued enough by that to read the rest of it?

In Stamford, Connecticut, I learned about the good, the bad, and the ugly. Put 'em together and what do you have? The Mafia. I met a Governor who I so pissed off that he said, "Young man, do you understand I could have you arrested before you even rose from your chair?" He didn't but he did scare the hell out of me. I also got shot at in Stamford, not by the Mafia mind you, but the Black Panthers. Churchill came to mind, "There is nothing so exhilarating than to be shot at—and realize they missed . . ."

I met heavy weight champ Floyd Patterson's sparring partner.

I did so because he thought his job shorted his pay, he broke into their offices, picked up their safe, and threw it into the wall of the building and onto the sidewalk. That is called prodigious strength.

I could go on—and I will. But it will take me about a year, so keep your eyes out for, "That's Why They Call It Work."

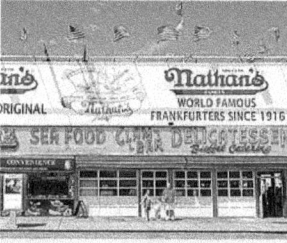

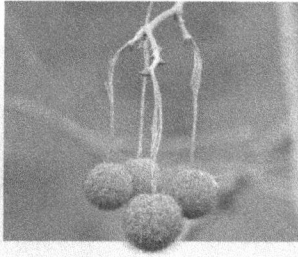

THE WAR OF THE
ITCHY BALLS

AND OTHER TALES FROM

Brooklyn

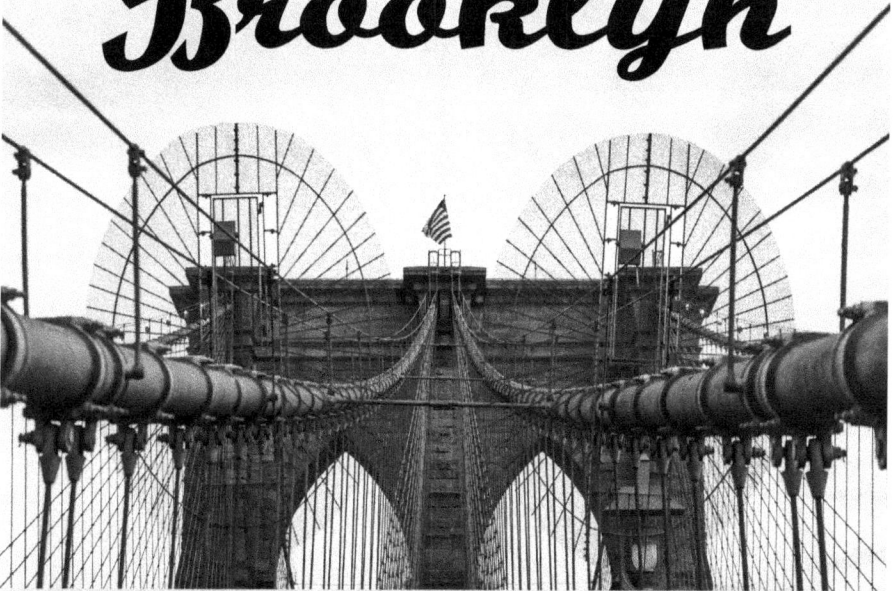

"If Brooklyn lore wasn't part of your life, it can be now." – Brian Williams, NBC News

A Half-Life Memoir by
WILLIAM A. GRALNICK

That's all folks!

For them as for us
There is nothing more beautiful
Than Memory

– Anonymous

The End